Syd Goldsmith's first taste of China's Cultural Revolution is blood on his tongue. It's 1967. Hong Kong is simmering, plagued by communist-led riots and strikes, crippled transport, punishing water-rationing, takeover threats from Beijing and roadside bombs. And Syd—the only Caucasian Foreign Service Officer at the American Consulate General who speaks Cantonese—is made responsible for reporting and analysis of the Hong Kong government's ability to survive.

The CIA station chief and the head of Macau's gold syndicate play major roles in Syd's story, along with *Newsweek's* Sydney Liu and Maynard Parker, and a steady stream of inquiring foreign correspondents and China-watchers. Richard Nixon makes a cameo appearance—to talk football with Syd since the consul general won't see him—in this riveting memoir of a year when Hong Kong's "borrowed time" seemed about to expire early.

Syd has been a diplomat, advisor to Chinese companies, concert flutist, and university professor during his forty years in Chinese places. He lives in Taipei with Hsiu-chen and their two children.

HONG KONG ON THE BRINK

by

Syd Goldsmith

BLACKSMITH BOOKS

HONG KONG ON THE BRINK

ISBN 978-988-77927-8-9 (paperback)
© 2017 Syd Goldsmith

Published by Blacksmith Books
Unit 26, 19/F, Block B, Wah Lok Industrial Centre,
31–35 Shan Mei St, Fo Tan, Hong Kong
www.blacksmithbooks.com

Typeset in Adobe Garamond by Alan Sargent
Printed in Hong Kong

First printing 2017

Contents

For all who would know that I lived

Acknowledgements

Good books are not likely to be what they are without help, and that certainly is the case with this memoir, as well as with my two novels, *Jade Phoenix* and *Two Musicians and The Wife Who Isn't.* I owe a debt of deep gratitude to readers and writers who were particularly helpful as I revised the manuscript numerous times and brought it to fruition.

Neal Moore, author of two memoirs, gave a tremendous amount of support and encouragement, as did James Spencer. They commented on all my drafts during this book's birthing process. Special appreciation to Genevieve Cimaz for her perspicacious and candid comments on this manuscript as well as on all my previous work. Thanks also to Patricia Averbach and Fred Zirm for their helpful suggestions, and to Alice O'Grady for her thoughts on an early effort.

I particularly appreciate the readings by Ambassador Burton Levin, and Allen Whiting, colleagues and mentors during 1967's heady days. They confirmed the facts of my account of how the Hong Kong crisis was handled in the

American Consulate General. Father Ron Saucci confirmed the accuracy of his role in the story. Nancy Zi amplified my understanding of the music scene in Hong Kong, so terribly important even though our musical life was all but suspended during the worst of the turmoil.

Literary agent Ken Sherman provided a reader's detailed commentary on the penultimate draft. Alan Sargent brought a deep understanding of history and a keen sense of words to the final edit for publication. Thanks go to Catherine Tai for a cover design that evokes a sense of the era.

I am hard put to find words sufficient to describe my publisher. Working with Pete Spurrier of Blacksmith Books is a writer's joy.

Special thanks to my wife, Chang Hsiu-chen, for her constant support as I relived a life in Hong Kong that was before her time.

CHAPTER I

Between Two Worlds

B Y CHINESE CULTURAL REVOLUTION standards Hong
Kong was tranquil. Rampaging Red Guards were not
fighting each other in the streets for dominance of chaos
they didn't understand. They weren't parading teachers in
front of their schools in dunce caps. They weren't sacking
the homes of class enemies, smashing every remnant of
culture they could get their hands on.

Hong Kong was refuge from all this, from the Civil War
and all the upheavals wreaked upon China by Mao. For
the colonials and the expats, it was the most exciting city
in the world, made so by stunning geography and wealth
built on the backs of dollar-a-day labor. And on the
extraordinary gap between the privileged elite and everybody else.

Set against events in the Mainland, two factory disputes
in the British colony were all but inconsequential to the
China watchers and most everybody else. They were modest
even in daily news value. I probably followed them closer
than most, since I was supposed to know what was going
on in Hong Kong. Although the small clusters of school
kids and workers waving their Little Red Books of Mao

thought at the factory gates caught my attention, it did not initially impress me as serious communist support for the aggrieved workers.

Snaking down Magazine Gap Road to Garden Road, it was impossible not to be aware of privilege. My Chevy Bel Air was a marker. If you owned a car, you were there. All those factories where workers festered and disputes were smothered by the smallest of management concessions were far away. We lived up on "The Peak." No factories there. Insulation. What's the big deal about a factory dispute?

Reeking of invulnerability, I went to my perch in the American Consulate General, confident of a bright future I had done little to earn besides passing a couple of tests. Success on the Foreign Service exams brought me to Hong Kong as a diplomat, and good fortune led me to become the Hong Kong/Macau political officer, responsible for reporting on domestic developments in the two colonies.

That afternoon of May 11, 1967 Allen Whiting called me up to the front office. "Why not take a stroll around the resettlement areas and those factories so you can do a firsthand report of the atmospherics?" A simple request, from the deputy chief of mission.

I wasn't too keen about that. Westerners weren't known for strolls in the resettlement estates, unless they were a police officer leading a platoon of Chinese cops. The recent Steve McQueen film *The Sand Pebbles* brought shivers at the thought of being skinned alive by an angry Chinese mob.

My desire to please a patron who had taken me on as a protégé struggled mightily with my jitters. I wasn't one to contradict my mother either. I kept my reservations to myself.

Better to take on this assignment with a Chinese companion who knew his way around. I called Sydney Liu of *Newsweek*'s Hong Kong Bureau.

At his suggestion, we headed toward the Tung Tau Resettlement Estate, a sprawling complex of twelve-story buildings allotting twenty-four square feet of living space for each squatter that the Hong Kong government (HKG) moved from hillside shacks into housing. The estate abutted Kowloon Walled City, a lawless warren run by criminal gangs. Close by the far side of the resettlement complex was the site of the dispute, an artificial flower factory fitting tight into a dreary scene.

We walked down a main thoroughfare edging the estate buildings on one side and a concrete expanse awaiting development on the other. Dusk settled in. We took in our surroundings in whispers, with the premonition that the conversation of outsiders could be the spark that sets off an explosion.

Trash fires sprang up out of nowhere; cardboard cartons alight, then tires thrown into bonfires. Quicker than letting out school, a large crowd poured out of the estate buildings, flooding the street and the paved lot on the other side.

Sydney Liu and I were surrounded and challenged before we could back away. *"Faan gwai lo!"* Shouts in the darkness.

Encroaching night gave no protection from being recognized as Caucasian. This was not an area where foreigners came to watch the sunset. Police patrols known for taking bribes were occasionally accompanied by a British officer in on the take; such was the white man's presence. Prohibitions on hawking and other unlicensed efforts of hungry people to make a living on the streets led to fines, bribery, and resentment of police interference in their grimy affairs.

"Faan gwai lo," literally "Troublesome foreign devil" was a common term describing foreigners in Hong Kong, but never had it been hurled at me like this. "Run for your life" was the message. I could only hope the snarling faces would taste triumph in my fear and let me flee.

Wrong. In seconds. Cacophony of curses. One I understood—*baak pei jyu*—white-skinned pig.

As many people who could closed in, pressed hard against my back and chest and pummeled. The rank just behind them shoved and stretched out to get in a blow. Somebody yelled, "Cop!"

"No. Not a cop!" I shouted.

A tug on my shirt then the pull and rip. The assailants pushed so hard to get at me they couldn't free their arms enough to strike a solid blow. Fists landed, but I would have been propped up even if knocked out. No room to fall. Only pain.

"I'm not police. I'm a missionary studying Cantonese." They pounded my shoulders and cursed. Drew salt blood from a cut lip. I tried to cover my face with my arms. Much of me protected by the crush of the crowd. Fists flailed. They only hurt so much. Lucky the crowd pressed in so close. Still conscious. Pummeling I would never forget. Maybe not badly hurt. "I'm a missionary. Please."

Was it an argument that developed among some of my attackers? Howls drowned out the details. More shouting. Helpless. Leadership emerged. The strikers closest to me stopped. "We should let him go." Five or six men took charge and formed a V in front of me. "Follow." They plowed through the crowd. Left me some distance away. Dazed and desperate to be somewhere else.

Cut tongue, garnished with blood and salt. Shirt ripped hanging loose. Wallet still bulging in my pocket. Mob not robbers. Get a cab, a bus, get out of here. Desolate deserted road.

Some distance on I hailed a cab. It slowed to a halt in front of me. Stares. I approached to open the door. The driver took off. No blood on his back seat. Keep on going. Another taxi sped away as I flailed at it. I ran after it, yelling *"Gauh meng ah!*— Help!"

What had happened to Sydney? I lost sight of him when I broke and ran from the mob. Need him now. Alone, not quite running, not quite walking. Emptiness.

Until I turned to look back where I came from. In the distance people were running in my direction. No idea how many, how many seconds before I heard the screaming. Fright becomes icy shivers. Goosebumps. No place to hide. Getting closer.

A space between buildings. Maybe a foot and a half wide. Wedged myself in sideways. Scraped an elbow. Turned my shoulders to the walls. Faced the street. Shudder in the heat. At least it would be one on one. Two couldn't get to me unless one stood on the shoulders of the other.

Howling chorus of a stampeding mob. Almost on top of me now. Brace! Brace!

CHAPTER 2

Serendipity

NO RHYME NOR REASON explains how it came about that I was a newly minted Foreign Service Officer (FSO) assigned to the American Consulate General in Hong Kong in 1965.

Had I not listened to my parents' advice to finish college before making career decisions, I would have asked for leave from Columbia in 1958 while still a junior, to become the assistant to the principal flutist of the New Jersey Symphony. My passion for music probably meant that I would have been deliriously happy earning the princely sum of $2,000 a year, never to return to that ivy-laced path to prestigious employment.

Were it not for a casual stroll across campus with the unremembered college classmate who asked, "Why don't you take the Foreign Service Officer exam next month?" I would not have been aware it was being offered. Thanks for setting me on a path I would follow for thirty years.

That written test was much like the Scholastic Aptitude Test taken by college-bound high school students. Montclair High gave me advantages taking those kinds of tests. It was considered to be the best public school in New Jersey, good enough to get me accepted into Harvard, but another test led me to Columbia. The navy offered a full tuition scholarship there, plus a $50 monthly stipend and an officer's commission upon graduation. I didn't have it in me to ask my parents to pay for Harvard when I had won a free ride to a top college.

The written Foreign Service test was just another exam in the testing universe. Surviving the orals was another matter entirely. I was just twenty-one, and the average age of candidates actually entering the Foreign Service was ten years older. The winnowing process was said to be excruciating. I was told that some 36,000 candidates took the written test in 1959. Depending on the budget, about one in eight were offered the oral assessment in those years. Approximately 500 of the original candidates would be placed on the register and 100 to 150 eventually would become FSOs. Many career officers were only hired after years of trying.

I had three months to agonize about the oral exam, scheduled for March, 1960. I knew almost nothing about the wider world beyond staring stupefied at Sputnik from the corner of Broadway and 116th Street in October 1957. I didn't read a newspaper. I didn't read *Time* or *Life*. Perhaps the best benefit of my college education was realization that my only hope was to get The News of the Week in Review section of the Sunday *New York Times*. My parents subscribed. I read it voraciously those thirteen weeks. I tried to memorize all the news fit to print and almost forgot about flute practice, though I was still taking lessons with the late great Julius Baker.

When I went into the small room of some nondescript government office building for that oral exam, the three senior officers who were to decide my fate were cordial enough. One enjoyed the upper-crust name "Donovan Quay Zook" that still sticks in my mind. Another such memorable FSO was quoted in *Time* (November 30, 1962) as saying, "I am the sixth Outerbridge Horsey and my unhappy son is the seventh. In fact, the only trouble with any new post is explaining the name to people."

I wondered how Sydney Goldsmith could mix with those names. Mr. Zook asked how I felt about working with people of different religions and cultures. Lucky for me. "My high school friend, Roger Bove, brought me into the Young People's Fellowship of the Episcopal Church in Montclair, and I was soon offered the presidency. I never understood why because I'm Jewish and everybody knew it." I couldn't miss the surprised looks on my inquisitors' faces, so I added, "I think I can work with anyone."

The other two examiners were the hatchet men. "Would you assign a black as an ambassador to a black African country?" Why or why not? What considerations? Then there were the rat-a-tat machine-gun questions about anything and everything. The best answers I could come up with most of the time were "I don't really know, but I would speculate. . . ."

By the time the two-hour grilling was over I didn't want to smell anything near my armpits. I was certain to be told to try again when I knew something about the real world. "Have a seat outside please." In those days candidates were told on the spot whether they passed the oral assessment.

I was free to chew my fingernails for as long as it took the three examiners to conclude that I didn't make the cut.

I chewed as my guts grumbled for well over an hour. The examiners came out the door deadpan and approached the bench where I sat. "Congratulations." They offered their hands in turn. "Next step is the security clearance and then you will be put on the register, with a deferral for your navy service." I could barely mumble some words of thanks.

It seemed so arbitrary that I passed the orals the first try. Were they looking for a few younger FSOs? Was it because I expressed pride about becoming a navy officer when few were serving? Was the Foreign Service looking for some Jewish candidates to parry charges of anti-Semitism? My parent's friends asked how such a nice Jewish boy could even consider joining the Foreign Service; it was so anti-Semitic, guilty of turning away desperate Jews fleeing the Nazis.

Those of you who needed a security clearance for a government job know that the process can be daunting. First, there is the "statement of personal history." List all residences and schools you attended from 1 January 1937. I was born in 1938. I couldn't provide a 1942 Richmond, Virginia address in 1960. I couldn't name the elementary school I attended in Jamaica, New York from 1943 to 1946.

The amount of juvenile information required for an adult security clearance was less than amusing. Good thing my parents were still alive and able to help.

More striking was the kind of information the special agents sought and the amount of time they devoted to the task. All our neighbors were interviewed and asked whether there was any indication that I might be a homosexual. By the time I was finally cleared, nine months had passed. I had been in the navy with secret clearance for much of that time.

That wasn't the end of it. After almost three years of service in the navy and top-secret clearance as a cryptography officer, I was offered appointment in the Foreign Service in April 1963—subject to a renewal of my clearance. I still have a carbon copy of a deposition I gave at the State Department Office of Security in New York on June 17, 1963, after it was "brought to my attention by Special Agent HANREHAN that, during interview by the Department of State representative at Athens, Georgia, on October 26, 1960, I am reported to have stated that I was never approached regarding a homosexual act to my knowledge. The date of said interview was subsequent to the first incident which I have related in my statement of June 4, 1963, as having occurred in the summer of 1959."

I had been approached at Columbia's West End Bar and shoved my harasser off his bar stool, and again on a bus returning from navy training. Both times I was in uniform. I categorically denied active or passive participation in any sort of homosexual activity, and offered to submit to a polygraph examination.

To my surprise, the security clearance came through much faster this time. President Johnson's facsimile signature certified that he appointed me as a Foreign Service Officer in September, 1963, less than three months after my sworn declaration of heterosexual propriety. Perhaps that certificate will become a collector's item a century from now, because President Kennedy was still alive and in office that September.

As a result of another one of those tests for nerds, the State Department offered me an immediate leave of absence to attend Columbia's Russian Institute on a National Defense Foreign Language Fellowship. With intensive Russian training and a graduate degree before I would even start working with State, there wasn't a shadow of doubt that I would become a Cold War specialist in Soviet affairs.

By the time I finally came on active duty in the Foreign Service in April 1965, five years had gone by since I'd passed the oral exam at the age of twenty-one. In the interim, I had served in the navy, been through the Cuban Missile Crisis, gotten a Master's degree in Russian history and—expecting an overseas assignment—set a June 13th wedding date to Barbara Blaker. She was a nurse introduced by her classmate, my cousin Sharon. My mother, always hinting that it was time to get married, was ecstatic.

I doubt that Barbara was aware of how deep a void she had to fill. I had loved Peggy Strum ever since she was thirteen and I was seventeen, for nearly ten years. She had loved me too, coming to see me in Montclair under the pretext of visiting my sister Linda. We read the comics together in bed, innocently. It was in the days before birth control, when I was keenly aware of statutory rape, proven by pregnancy. More, I strongly believed in protecting the girl I would marry, which meant clothes on. True to the double standard, girls I would never consider marrying were fair game during that period I was waiting for Peggy to come of age.

We didn't really date until she was a senior in high school and I a senior in college. Could there have been any doubt where we were headed when I asked her what she wanted for her birthday that November and she said, "To be engaged." We didn't need to announce it. All who knew us were certain we would marry someday. We were all over each other on the benches in Riverside Park, clothes still on.

I loved her so deeply—but not so desperately as to overcome my fear that the exorbitant cost of long-distance telephone calls from the Navy Supply School in Athens, Georgia to her home in Brooklyn would swallow my entire ensign's pay of $222.30 a month. Had I called as often as I wanted to talk, it would have cost much more than that.

So I assumed that she would understand and we would pick up our love when I returned for Thanksgiving. I didn't call that summer. To this day I do not really understand why I was so stupid.

Peggy didn't want to continue that fall. She would give no reason. I had no capacity to understand how she had felt all that summer. She never let me see her again. Five years loved, five years lost. Still trying to bury the pain when Barbara came along.

Only navy discipline kept me from alcohol and drugs. Some sense of pride that I did not need help kept me from being overwhelmed by depression that would not go away. I took what little advantage I could of the brainy but prudent graduate-school girls I met during my stint at Columbia's Russian Institute. Their bright babble turned me off. My devastating loss of Peggy left no room to accept them for who they were.

Barbara came along as an amiable and good companion, largely because she didn't annoy me with idle talk and accepted any activity that I proposed. Then there was my mother's subtle influence in the background. Endless praise for this lovely Jewish girl. It's time to take a wife. You don't want to be alone. Not in some faraway place like Hong Kong.

It came to be that I convinced myself that I loved or accepted Barbara enough to have her be my bride. My best man would be beside himself that he was unable to stop me from staring out at Tamiment Lake that wedding day until I was twenty minutes late for the ceremony.

Once we were engaged, Barbara moved in with her "knight in shining armor"—me—and three other guys who shared a rental house in the nation's capital while I went to the A-100 initiation course for new FSOs. She waited for me to come home and cooked while I was indoctrinated in the ways of the Foreign Service. We studied strange cultures, foreign gestures, and driving techniques to break away from a kidnap attempt.

Towards the end of the course we were interviewed about our interests and assignment preferences. Mine were obvious. The personnel officer gave every appearance of being attentive and sympathetic to my request for assignment to Moscow.

He waited until I finished talking about my aspirations to become a Soviet expert. Then he spoke, "We don't send first-tour officers to Russia. We have more Soviet experts than we will ever need, and you wouldn't like the pecking order anyway. Now where do you want to go?"

I was still trying to collect myself when he added an explanation. "The Russians are expert at exploiting our frailties. An attractive woman entices a young married FSO and he will do anything to avoid having his infidelity exposed, because it's the end of his career and probably his marriage too. Blackmail works even better with homo-sexuals. Maybe you heard about Guy Burgess and Donald Maclean, the British double agents who fled to Russia. We have our cases too, so where would you like to go?"

I hadn't given a thought to alternatives. Where had I been? To Guantanamo Bay, Istanbul, Catania, San Remo, and Bastia on the USS *Bristol,* DD 857, a World War II destroyer that was my shipboard home in the navy. "What about Japan?" I asked.

The personnel officer sized me up. "You look more like a Chinese type than a Japanese type to me. What would you think of an assignment to Taipei, or possibly Hong Kong with some Cantonese language training?"

I didn't know anything about either of those places, so, "It sounds fine to me."

Steve Lesser got the assignment to Japan while I was assigned to Hong Kong. Steve had struck me as quite shy during the course of our training, almost reticent. Later I learned that he had the right kind of reserve for Japan and I did not. I was much more suited to serve in Chinese cultures. I never learned whether the personnel officer was prescient about these personality traits or just filling a roster of job vacancies.

This was an assignment for which I had absolutely no background or qualifications. I didn't know any Chinese and hadn't taken a single course on China in college or graduate school. My only feel for China was my mother's admonitions during World War II. "Millions of Chinese children are starving. Finish up all the food on your plate."

I can still wonder what rhyme or reason led me to Hong Kong in 1965 . . . and now forty years living in Chinese places.

CHAPTER 3

Musical Honeymoon

I COULD NOT HAVE IMAGINED what I would be getting into, both before and after that day in May 1967 when I cowered in fear of an early obituary.

The briefing papers I read in Washington in 1965 said nothing about the Cultural Revolution. Though Hong Kong was the epicenter of our efforts to gain intelligence about China, there was no hint of the paroxysms of violence that would soon engulf China for a decade. If you believe that all the king's horses and all the king's men are unable to predict cataclysmic upheavals, this was a good example.

Least of all could I conceive of Hong Kong under attack by Red Guard–inspired leftists. About half the population of nearly four million had fled the Chinese Civil War or subsequent upheavals. Hong Kong was refuge. For communist China, it was the goose that laid the golden egg. Trade with and through Hong Kong was the PRC's largest source of hard currency. There was no thought that the British authority there might be challenged or forced to kowtow or abandon the colony. The most I could claim as a prognosticator was that Hong Kong was achieving a degree of success by transforming itself into a free-trade manufacturing center for export of cheap labor-intensive goods like textiles and plastic flowers.

This would be an orientation and training assignment. I would be rotated among the four functional cones of the Foreign Service: political, economic, consular, and administrative; four to six months for each. The personnel people had agreed that it might be a good idea to have a Caucasian FSO in the consulate general who could speak the local dialect. I would get six months of Cantonese language training.

Before setting off for Hong Kong, I was treated to a two-month stint on the German Desk in the State Department. The desks are where we coordinate all aspects of relations with other countries. The assignment would have been unremarkable save for a request from the German Foreign Ministry for clarification of an unsourced news report that Senator Warren Magnuson (D-Washington) intended to visit China. Since travel there was prohibited, did that signal a change in US policy to isolate the communist regime?

My reply would need appropriate clearances. I went around asking questions of people who would send me on to other people; on and on to people who felt obliged to express concern and their importance in the clearance process. Views ranged from, "That's impossible," to "The senator is a nutcase communist who always wanted to go to China." Twenty-six initialed clearances later, I had achieved a one-sentence consensus response: "We have no information concerning Senator Magnuson's plans about a possible visit to China."

That's how I learned why the State Department was called the Fudge Factory. The experience had a profound influence. I shunned country desk jobs throughout my entire Foreign Service career, sometimes kicking patrons in the teeth by declining pleas to follow in their footsteps.

Most useful during that temporary stint in Washington, I learned that I could travel by ship to Hong Kong on my government orders without being charged leave for all those days at sea. Though air travel was readily available, we had the option to take this boondoggle. For Barbara and me, it would be our honeymoon, since I was allowed only one day off from the A-100 training course when we were married.

Regardless of rank, the regulations allowed minimum available first-class passage. The American President Lines people knew just how to handle those government bookings. Take note of the request and delay the reservation formalities until the last minute. That allowed non-government passengers to book the cheaper first-class staterooms and left the really expensive luxury travel to feed off the government teat. We were booked into a lovely stateroom on the upper deck of the SS *President Wilson,* with an ocean view and a rather large invoice to the State Department.

This was an extraordinary subsidy for American President Lines and a big gift to us. The seventeen-day voyage across the Pacific from San Francisco to Hong Kong counted as on-duty travel time and amounted to more paid leave than I would earn in a year.

The *President Wilson* started life as a planned World War II troop transport, but construction was canceled in December 1944. It was completed and chartered to American

President Lines in 1948, to become a luxury liner for round-the-world cruises.

The *Wilson*'s 18,962 gross tons and 609-foot length looked very impressive compared to the 2,200-ton destroyer that was my previous seafaring experience. The USS *Bristol* (DD 857) had five-inch-gun mounts. The SS *President Wilson* had two swimming pools and a deck where you could walk most of the circumference of the ship all day long. As a navy supply officer, I knew the allowed expenditure was $1.09 per day per sailor for three meals. There was no limit to how much you could eat on the *Wilson*—prime rib, gravy-soaked mashed potatoes, baked Alaska, delicacies even sweeter.

Whether hungry or not, Barbara and I stuffed ourselves as a matter of shipboard routine. Gluttony at the troth, calories savored. With the cooperation of a Pacific Ocean as smooth as our porcelain tableware, we kept all those glorious meals down. It showed.

But we could only eat, drink, walk the decks, play shuffleboard, see the shows and stay in bed so many hours a day. We didn't socialize a lot and kept pretty much to ourselves. I didn't use the library either, betraying avoidance of reading as leisure. I didn't even bring any books about Hong Kong, complacent that I had read the briefing papers in Washington. There would be plenty of time to learn about Hong Kong once I got there.

I sensed beforehand that seventeen days at sea with no responsibility for the ship could present a serious challenge to a former navy seafarer. Though this was to be a honeymoon trip, my thoughts on filling the days turned inevitably to the flute and music. Between the demands of new employment in the Foreign Service and Barbara's move-in, I had hardly touched the instrument in months. I couldn't help but brood on how many times one of the great passions of my life ended before it even started.

By 1951 I had already given up two instruments and gotten a D in Mr. Pinter's required eighth-grade music class. The three classmates who joined me to haul the classroom door out of school, across the street past the Carnegie Library and up Bellevue Avenue past a row of elegant houses turned into professional offices all got Fs. Maybe the D was because I was more musical than my friends and otherwise kept my mouth shut. They merit most of the credit for driving our hapless music teacher to the nuthouse.

Not long after that I was standing anxious before Antonio Sant Ambrogio, a stern wiry man with a bristly mustache, a stubble garden on his cheeks and a cigarette in his mouth.

"Why do you want to take violin lessons?" he asked.

His voice wasn't harsh, but his intense dark eyes under heavy brows made me feel very small. I looked away, towards the grand piano that dominated the dimly lit living room. An open violin case, two bows and some music labeled Beethoven were on the lid. A cello case sat against the wall under a picture of a symphony orchestra.

"I need to have some culture," I said, repeating the explanation my parents gave for bringing me here.

Mr. Sant Ambrogio asked my age. Thirteen. "You're too old to begin violin lessons."

For a second, the scene froze in place: stern teacher, spurned student, stunned parents.

My father, who took violin lessons until he was almost seventeen, broke the silence. "Why?"

"Because he won't learn to play well enough before graduation to appreciate the music, so he'll give it up the minute he leaves high school, if not sooner."

Before any of us could understand why a music teacher was turning away a student, Mr. S continued. "It is possible to learn to play the flute well enough in a few years to want to continue. When I was in the Saint Louis symphony before the War, I took some lessons from the principal flutist. Georges Barrère was the best of his era. I can teach your son the flute."

My first assignment as a new flutist was to blow across the lips of coke bottles until Mr. S could procure an instrument for me. "Make a good sound," he said. "If you want to create a scale and play a tune, take eight bottles and fill them with different levels of water to make an octave."

I liked that idea. Eight bottles of coke just for me, but my parents nixed that. "One bottle will be sufficient for you to perfect your tone. You can fill it to different levels and experiment."

Before my next lesson dad presented me with a shiny new silver-plated Armstrong flute. "It cost $138, so you should practice a little every day." That sounded expensive to this thirteen year old, but serious flutists think about instruments at car prices, and string players compare the price of their dream instrument to the cost of a mansion.

It was only a few weeks before Mr. S made it clear that I should be practicing a lot more than that little bit every day. He would stand beside me with a conductor's baton over my head and say, "We do *solfeggio* first. Now *do-re-mi-fa-sol-la-si-do*. If the note is *la* you say *la*. In tempo now. Get the rhythm right. No. That's a dotted quarter. Again." He would tap the grand piano with the baton and clap time. I couldn't keep up with him.

Eventually Mr. S would stop clapping, stare straight at me until I became very small, and ask, "Did you practice this like I told you to?" Silence. "You don't know how to count. You won't understand the music or play it right if you don't do *solfeggio*." Clap clap clap. "One two three. In time now."

Looking back from the perspective of my honeymoon on the *Wilson,* I realized that he was trying with a passion bordering on desperation to teach this lazy Goldsmith kid to be a flutist.

On our second day at sea I left Barbara basking in the sunshine on the Promenade deck, went back to our gorgeous minimum-available first-class stateroom, and took my flute out of a suitcase to see if I could revive my on-again off-again love affair with the instrument and its music. It was only a few minutes before determination to show that Mr. S had not failed grabbed me and held sway over the voyage.

CHAPTER 4

New Beginnings

WE ARRIVED IN HONG KONG on a bright clear day in October, 1965. Traversing the harbor, I gaped at a city of downtown skyscrapers and too-tall apartment buildings on stilts shimmering in the sun. They seemed to be supported by toothpick pillars seeking a foundation, teetering on the almost cliffs leading to Victoria Peak. I wondered if they would come tumbling down like pick-up-sticks. Later I would see that devastation when it happened. A twelve-story apartment building on a steep hillside collapsed in a typhoon in 1968, giving James Clavell inspiration for a grisly description in *Noble House,* his historical novel about two venerable trading houses vying for dominance in the British colony. When I finally got to read it, the finely woven story gave a better feel for the place and its history than government briefing papers ever had.

Harold Christie waved to us on the gangplank and introduced himself as our welcoming party. He was a rather corpulent consul in his fifties, immaculately dressed, with slicked-back black hair and a shiny smile. In different attire he would have made an ideal Santa Claus. Jolly in voice, he bore the gifts of instant welcome and engagement. More to me than to Barbara, as usual in the men's world of the day. Barbara didn't seem to mind listening to us talk. That's what attracted me to her when we first met.

We were still walking along the wharf of Ocean Terminal when he asked, "What do you like to do in your free time?" It was as if that was the most important thing on earth for him and he knew it was for me too.

"I studied flute with Julius Baker. He's the principal in the New York Philharmonic."

Of course I was not posted to Hong Kong as a musician, though Hal Christie made it sound like I was. Here was Hal talking about concerts instead of my orientation stints in the consular, administrative, economic and political sections.

Hal made it his mission to make us comfortable. He and a local assistant would not let us carry anything as they struggled to get our baggage to the car. We strolled by the China Goods store opposite the Kowloon Star Ferry pier. Hal pointed us towards a window displaying exquisite jade carvings of women in flowing gowns and obese Buddhas who seemed to be accompanying them. "You can go in there and see precious ivory, jade and coral that's beautiful beyond belief, but we can't buy any of it. If it looks Chinese and you don't have a certificate of origin to prove it was made in Hong Kong you're a criminal." He paused, shielded his mouth with his hand, and then whispered, "Americans can't buy Chicom goods but some people get away with it."

Then he sent the driver ahead. "You'll like this much better than riding in a station wagon." We walked toward the ferry terminal and joined the stream of commuters and tourists heading for the Victoria Harbor crossing. "Have a look at this incredible place," said Hal. "That clock tower over there is the train station. Walk a minute and you could get on a train to China, if only we were allowed to. Right behind where we came from you're on the ship back to San Francisco or you could go around the world. This is the incredible Star Ferry. Looks like we'll be on the *Radiant Star* to weave between more ships than you can count on the way across the most beautiful harbor in the world."

We watched a couple of deckhands tie the ferry up to the chocks, drop the gangplank and pull it up again in hardly a minute. Out past the pier I started to count sampans, junks and freighters and couldn't count nearly fast enough. Hal was right. How they were able to avoid collisions was beyond me.

When we got to the Hilton Hotel, Hal presented Barbara with flowers. Next day I would be introduced to the administrative section. Barbara could enjoy the shops and the swimming pool in the hotel while I took care of all the paperwork.

Hal had already told me that I would start out working in the consular section. It seemed a bit strange, but I held my questions for the administrative officer. When we met I asked when I could expect to start language training. "There's been a bit of a delay in that. The program at New Asia College won't have teachers available for you until January, when some of the missionaries graduate. Don't worry. You won't be studying Bible." With that he turned me over to a local employee to check in.

Forms dominated the day; forms to record my arrival and assignment, to get paid, for withholding taxes, for a driver's license for the left side of the road, to establish identity as an accredited US diplomat. Then there were forms to determine allowances, clear household effects through customs, and assign housing.

"Unfortunately there is no housing available at the moment." With no hint of apology, another administrative officer said we would be housed for a short while at the Hilton, where I left Barbara that morning. The hotel was a short walk down the hill from the consulate general. "It's very nice and quite a bargain for Uncle Sam at twelve dollars a night. You'll find that life is much cheaper here." I did a quick calculation that the government would be paying an amount greater than half my salary to house us in the Hilton until they could move us into somewhere.

I was soon to discover that housing was tighter for most everybody in Hong Kong than the briefing papers suggested. The government could not come close to building resettlement estates fast enough to house the refugees from the Civil War and the upheavals that marked the Mao regime. While some hillsides hosted skyscrapers others were teeming with thousands of squatters. Apartments that met decent standards were in such high demand that the consulate's administrative staff had to scramble to rent suitable lodging for the burgeoning staff.

We were to stay at the Hilton for three months. By any standard this two-year-old property was luxurious. It was the only five-star hotel on the Hong Kong side of the harbor. I would take a swim in the outdoor pool early in the morning and walk to work. Barbara sometimes joined for the swim. The temporary per diem allowance was sufficient to allow us to eat in the hotel or in the classy restaurants a short walk away in the Central District.

Those restaurants were a gourmet's paradise at food-stamp prices. Delicacies like beggar's chicken and shark's fin were within our budget. We had Peking duck, tea duck, camphor duck, pressed Chiu-chow duck, and more kinds of chicken, fish, and pork than we could count. The array of sauces boggled. Menus offered hundreds of dishes. You could look at the pictures all evening without being able to choose among the delicacies if a waiter didn't come around and do it for you.

When gourmandize became more than we could eat, all we had to do was wander into a nearby alley or over to Western Market and order dumplings or noodles for pocket change. Sometimes we took the Star Ferry to Kowloon to savor that extraordinary harbor crossing. We soon discovered there were hundreds of restaurants just a short walk from the terminal. What better way to start a new life in a strange land?

But I had failed to consider that while I was at work, the Hilton probably was a cage for Barbara, surrounded by a maze packed with people speaking strange tongues. My good wife did not complain. "Sort of interesting but I can't understand a thing except in the stores for the English."

For nearly three months Barbara said nothing about her solitude when we shared those splendid sheets in the Hilton. I would leave her to swim laps early in the morning, then make my way up Garden Road to the squat four-story building that housed the American Consulate General, aspiring to get on with life as a diplomat representing exceptional America, the most powerful country in the history of the world.

As the maximum ninety days of per diem allowance for temporary lodging was about to expire, we were moved to a comfortable two-bedroom apartment on Coombe Road, a quiet side street on the way up to Victoria Peak. It was no more than a fifteen-minute drive from the office, but the area gave no hint that the teeming tenement districts characteristic of most of the colony were only minutes away. Our apartment would not have been considered luxurious in the United States, but the average Hong Kong white-collar worker in the 1960s could not imagine living on Coombe Road.

Years later I reflected back on the squatter settlements and resettlement estates that were squalid reality when I served there. Never would I make a claim of writing good poetry, but I share this impression of life in Hong Kong for the multitudes who had fled disasters in China.

> Endless blocks occluding view
> Lego-like, dripping black moss
> of tropical pigeon-do
> Not real estate but quiet
> Desperation
>
> Escarpment housing
> hordes of tattered
> shards of Mao Tse-tung
> perched on cliff sides
> Clinging

Forced from mud-slide precipice
squished in this new steaming hell
respite from civil ravage
China wars a constant smell
Refuge

Space planned with painful scruples
one hundred twenty square feet
for five souls built in great haste
like sneaked love noble intent
Home

How much is that allotment?
Twenty-four square feet for one
sleeping soul on coarsest slats
Tiny shelves below the bunks
hold lives of snoring strangers
Tattered

Where homeless others still live
three shifts for each tatami
share eight hours solitude
Four other disembodies
each living silent nightmares
and unbounded aspiration
Elsewhere

CHAPTER 5

Cat and Mouse

MY FIRST TRAINING ASSIGNMENT was in the immigrant visa section. Once all my forms were filled out, Hal Christie took me to meet the consular affairs section chief.

Mr. Farnsworth was a lean angular man nearing sixty who came to be remembered best for the operation to remove his fungus-infected toenails and its painful aftermath. Translated from the Cantonese, they called it Hong Kong foot, which often turned out to be a lifelong toenail challenge punctuated by periodic invasions of *tinia pedis* between the toes.

The polite questions faded quickly from memory, but not what followed. Mr. Farnsworth took a picture from his desk and asked me if I noticed anything strange. It was an 11x14 inch formal portrait of what seemed to be a typical stiff-posed Chinese family. The almost scowling grandparents were positioned on a pedestal, seated in traditional blackwood chairs above their descendants. They stared straight out, as if suspicious that a poltergeist lurking inside the camera would steal their souls. The clench-lipped children with their spouses were lined up in a stilted row below them, in chairs without armrests. Grandchildren were set stone-like, squatting below their parents' platform.

Mr. Farnsworth didn't give me much time to reflect. "Well. Do you see anything unusual about this photograph?"

I looked at it closely, but not closely enough.

"Count the legs," said Mr. Farnsworth.

I was puzzled. "Look closely." There it was, an extra leg in the row of adult children, crowded between two seated men notable for their identical blank stares.

"This is just one example of the lengths these people go to get into the US by posing as the son of an American citizen. They buy their identity."

Mr. Farnsworth explained that doctored photos were just one facet of widespread immigration fraud. "With an annual immigration quota of only 100 for China and other Asian countries, what goes on here is no surprise. Except for spouses and children of citizens, an intending immigrant could wait much longer than a lifetime and still not get a visa.

"We're vitally important to these people. They've plotted and paid for their immigration long in advance. Sometimes decades. For them, we are a hostile barrier to their desperate illegal ambition. For us it's the last bastion of defense against fraud."

We left Mr. Farnsworth in his office to nurse his toenails. Hal took me on a tour of the first floor and called it the most interesting place in the world to do visa work. American consuls and local employees devoted to deciphering immigration files and searching for fraud were arrayed at desks neatly arranged in compact rows. Applicants for immigration were interviewed out in the open. Sweat on lips and suppressed tremors confirmed that they were very nervous.

The American consuls guarding the immigration gates should have been nervous too. They were totally dependent on the local national clerks and translators. None of them could speak or understand more than the most rudimentary Cantonese.

I learned during that introduction that male Chinese-American citizens saved for years to go back to their villages in Kwangtung province where they immediately married if they had not left a wife behind when they emigrated. They usually stayed about a year, and every such visit resulted in a duly recorded birth of a baby boy. If the father could afford to stay long enough, he claimed two boys, one after the other. These "births" were recorded in the traditional family register of births, marriages and deaths. The documents always showed male children, regardless of whether the child was a girl or there was no child at all.

For much of the first half of the twentieth century the family registers were also accepted by US authorities as evidence of the birth of a "son" of an American citizen born overseas. The creation of documented sons of American citizens in the rural areas near Canton occurred with impressive regularity during China's unceasing turmoil. Girls had no chance of immigrating to America's "Gold Mountain." Their births weren't registered. For immigration purposes they did not exist.

Genuine sons thus had a path to immigration, but the real value of those registered male births to an American citizen father was as evidence to support a fraudulent claim to citizenship. Demand far exceeded supply. The false

papers were believed to command about $30,000, a prin-
cely sum for the purchaser in rural China. At the time that
was enough to buy six thirty-foot traditional Chinese
seafaring junks, or pay my salary for four years.

The applicants did not have the money, but there was
an intricate web of credit and loans. Normally these false
sons arrived at the Gold Mountain of their imagination
only to discover that they would be repaying their debts
with many years of indentured labor in Chinese restaurants
or sweatshops.

Adjudicating these immigration applications was a game
of cat and mouse. Consuls depended on locally hired staff
to investigate the truth behind the documents. Security
people were on alert for signs of bribery or fraud inside our
operation.

Some of the alleged sons were caught red-handed in their
fraud. Their assumed family names or village backgrounds
did not match what we knew from information compiled
by American advisors during World War II and the Chinese
Civil War. We had a handbook describing the villages in
Kwangtung province which accounted for the vast majority
of immigration fraud. Many of the isolated hamlets in the
Hoiping, Sun Wui and Toishan districts were populated
entirely by people surnamed Wong, or Chan, or Ng. If an
applicant named Cheung appeared at the consulate and
presented documents showing his birth to parents in a
village populated by Wong families, his application was
dead on arrival.

As we developed more information and ability to detect
fraud, Chinese immigration brokers became more adept at
avoiding detection. Their documentation matched

applicant's surnames with villages populated by people with the same name. Applicants were prepped with credible stories that were consistent with what we knew about their "home" villages. These sons could present family photos with the false father present each time he returned to China. Three-legged sons like the one I was shown were a rare mistake.

The effort to stem the fraud even included investigations of applicants' lodgings, which were often shared with strangers in tiny spaces. Our investigators tried to find out if an applicant was known by a name other than claimed on his application, or if he came from a different village than claimed.

I was taken on one of these investigations, to a resettlement estate featuring an endless row of twelve-story buildings built by the British colonial government in a massive effort to house the estimated 1.5 million refugees who had fled communist China. The refugees had doubled Hong Kong's population. In 1965 many were still living in shantytowns on terrain so steep that shacks washed down the hillsides whenever a typhoon hit.

These hastily constructed estates were so close to the airport that incoming planes cleared the rooftops by less than fifty feet on their circular approach over the Kowloon peninsula as they came in to land. I had the bad luck to be riding the upper level of a double-decker bus along the road fronting the runway when a 707 flew right overhead before burning rubber seconds later. I was scared shitless and seriously deaf for days. The horrifying consequences of a miscalculation skimming one of the most densely populated

cities in the world would have been rained on people who
fled one disaster only to die in another.

Each floor of typical resettlement housing consisted of
identical rows of 120-square-foot rooms facing a narrow
central corridor. Shared water, cooking and toilet facilities
were located at the end of the corridors. Five people were
allocated to each unit whether related or not.

Mr. Ng, our principal investigator, led me into one of
these cubby holes. We squeezed into a narrow space facing
the bunk beds piled atop each other almost from floor to
ceiling. I wondered how even two of the inhabitants could
possibly get into their bunks at the same time. Space for
personal belongings was little more than the equivalent of
today's airline carry-on bag. A frail old lady was sitting
hunched forward on the lowest bunk, knees drawn up to
her chest. She stared into space, cheeks hollow, lips tight.

The target of our investigation was not in. At first the
lady said nothing. Mr. Ng prodded. "Does he have family?"
She opened her lips just enough to say, "Don't know."

"Where did he come from?" The lady looked away. "No
idea."

Eventually she revealed that the applicant had been
living there for some time. She claimed to have no idea
about anything else. When we returned to the office Mr.
Ng answered my question. "Our visit produced no information that would contradict the applicant's story."

"I didn't understand a word, but it looks like the lady was
hiding something."

Mr. Ng looked at me dispassionately. "They all behave
that way when we ask questions. We can only guess."

That applicant was granted an immigration visa leading to likely servitude in the US for years. He could be expected to do whatever it takes to make a life better than he had in China and Hong Kong.

Buying fictitious paternity was already second- and third-generation fraud when I started interviewing applicants through an interpreter in the autumn of 1965. Our understanding of its extent was informed by a detailed study of Chinese immigration history prepared by a fellow Foreign Service officer, Leo J. Moser. Among other findings, he determined from examination of census and immigration records that there were 800 males claiming citizenship for each Chinese woman living in San Francisco at the time when their alleged birth records were lost during the 1906 earthquake and fire. As friends would tell me in Chinglish: "Chinese velly clever. Five thousand years culture. Outsmart foreign devils. Get to Gold Mountain."

CHAPTER 6

Goodbye Pravda

M Y PREPARATIONS for the Hong Kong assignment included a subscription to *Pravda,* for a year of news from Moscow at a ridiculously low price. I was cocksure my next post would be there, dealing with issues I knew something about. The State Department would not have allowed me a year and a half leave of absence to become a Soviet expert for nothing. I needed to keep up with developments in the USSR and maintain my proficiency in Russian. What better way than to get daily news and the language practice from the horse's mouth? Reading a few paragraphs of propaganda a day, I could almost call it a religious ritual.

"Pravda", literally translated, is "Truth." The Communist Party mouthpiece published what the dictatorship wanted people to know. American Kremlinologists might call it bullshit, but they read it word by word in the search for clues about Soviet leadership struggles, harvests, industrial production and other developments cloaked in veils of secrecy or mendacity. The most significant clue of all during my student days was the surprise capitalization of "First Secretary" that signaled the pending ascendancy of

Nikita Khrushchev. Few analysts of Soviet affairs picked up on such esoteric clues until after the fact. The more usual result of my reading *Pravda* was repeated confirmation that Moscow's "Truth" was synonymous with suspect facts and grinding boredom.

Though I only drifted into studying Russian in my senior year in college, graduate work in Columbia's Russian Institute made Kremlinology my métier. I felt compelled to read *Pravda* while I was adjudicating immigrant visa applications in Hong Kong, regardless of my disgust with communist gospel. I had drifted away from the doubts and insecurity of a career in music to the conviction that my Foreign Service career would be as a specialist in Soviet affairs. Yet here I was in Hong Kong, mesmerized by the vibrancy of its people and the sheer physical beauty of the place, of its *shan sui*; literally mountains and water. I also could not help but admire what I could see of the extra-ordinary efforts ordinary Chinese made to better their lives.

My disgust with *Pravda*'s gospel brought doubts about my career aspirations. In Hong Kong, other dreams started to take over. I would be studying Cantonese so I could speak to these people in their own language.

I was far from aware of all my dreams, but believed that dreams and compulsions come to the surface, disappear, and surface again after being dormant, sometimes for a very long time. It was that way with the flute. I had let it go many times, voluntarily or otherwise, and revived it again later. After a hiatus for the navy and another for the A-100 training course, I had learned a whole recital program aboard the *Wilson* with no idea when and where the opportunity would come to perform it. Though Harold

Christie had asked about my interests on the pier by the Star Ferry Terminal, that conversation had been put aside as I immersed myself in the hopes and fears of people who would jettison the lives they lived if only they could get to America.

After another day in visas, Hal came up to me and said he would introduce me to Arrigo Foa over the weekend. "Who is that?"

"Let it be a surprise. We'll meet here," said Hal.

Wiry, wizened, eyes shining with the fire of someone who had been through war and emerged barely alive, the conductor of the Hong Kong Symphony had taken Hal Christie's word about the American flutist. "You'll solo with the orchestra next month. I want you to play the Bach B minor Suite." Only then did he ask about my back-ground and reveal that he and most of the members of the orchestra were refugees from the Communist Revolution, fortunate to get out of China with their instruments. "Mr. Wong, the flutist, was a famous bamboo flute player in China before the War. You'll meet him at the rehearsal next week. He was the best in Shanghai, and learned Western flute there."

I had been in Hong Kong three months when a few words appeared in newspapers about the fine performance of the American flutist who had recently joined Hong Kong's musical community. I discovered that there wasn't a concert season as we know it. When the orchestra had a program ready, it arranged to perform in the City Hall Concert Hall and made the necessary announcements. Several months after my performance, Mr. Wong was featured playing the Mozart D Major Flute Concerto at the next concert, an evident salve to an ego badly bruised by the sudden appearance of that foreign flutist.

Music was alive and well, and so was the politics of it. Mr. Wong was prominent in the orchestra, well respected for his abilities in Chinese traditional music. I would go on to perform regularly in Hong Kong, but not again as soloist with the symphony.

In only a few months I had come to believe that Hong Kong was the most exciting city in the world. It wasn't just the music and the intrigue in all those visa applications. The stories people told about the upheavals they survived were as astounding as the beauty and the history of the place. *Pravda* notwithstanding, the truth was that I couldn't get enough of Hong Kong, and couldn't wait to start my language training.

That first day I took the Star Ferry across the harbor to Hung Hom and walked the streets to New Asia College to study Cantonese was the very last day I read *Pravda*. As I was told, "Cantonese language training is total immersion." I had no time for Soviet affairs. Lost interest quicker than I should admit. Never got to Russia. Can't speak even elementary Russian now.

No regrets.

CHAPTER 7

Amah Failure

B Y THE TIME I consigned *Pravda* to the trash we were reasonably well settled into our apartment on Coombe Road, though I knew the four neighbors who shared our building only in passing. One of them, a secretary who was about to leave for her next assignment, offered up her dog, a poodle mix we called Shu-shu.

Barbara broached another truth during a leisurely evening walk down our road of lush foliage to Wan Chai Gap. "It's time to get an amah. Everybody we've ever met says a household servant is essential and they're dirt cheap."

"But I thought you liked the adventure of going out and discovering everything on your own."

"I do. The markets are fascinating, but it gets creepy when all those men sweating in undershirts look at me funny and I can't understand what they say and I have no idea whether they're overcharging me. They slaughter the chickens and dangle them right in front of my nose. The women work even harder, chopping up slabs of pork, cleaning the chickens and pulling the guts out of the fish. They clean up the food stalls after the men too."

I knew that the local fresh food markets were exclusively Cantonese denizens, hundreds of small open stalls in old large public spaces. While a foreigner could survive by buying at expensive specialty shops catering to them, having an amah for shopping, cooking, cleaning and baby-sitting was the thing to do. Status was part of it. Colonials and expats trying to live life without Chinese help were looked upon as quirky or impoverished. The White Men were expected to support privileged wives who did not work.

"Are you sure you want to get an amah now rather than wait until we have children?"

"I didn't tell you before, but lately the neighbor has been taking me to Western Market with her amah. It's much easier that way, but it's not right to rely on her all the time."

"I see." We could afford to spend one twelfth of my salary to take a modest leap into the upper-crust life. Consulate colleagues said that the best way to find a good amah was ask somebody who was pleased with theirs. That somebody would talk to their amah, who would introduce a relative, or go to a friend who could. We would try that.

Our decision to hire an amah brought us a young girl who I didn't interview. At that time my beginner's Cantonese was far from good enough to carry on a decent conversation. I was happy to leave the choice to Barbara, who was the one who would have to live with the amah all day long while I was at New Asia College with a new teacher every hour.

Barbara told me after their meeting that this rather dumpy, very pimply young woman's command of English seemed even more elementary than my Cantonese. She couldn't ascertain the girl's age. "Did the girl say, 'I don't know' because she didn't want to reveal how young she was?" It seemed more likely that she didn't understand the question. Despite that, Barbara decided to try her out.

We had a month to decide whether to keep the new hire. If we were not satisfied, custom allowed the employer to let her go without severance or detectable rancor, even though there was quite a loss of face. If you decided to keep the amah after the first month, you were expected to employ her for as long as you remained in Hong Kong.

Barbara soon learned that it took more time and effort to get the girl to understand what needed to be done than it took to do the work herself. She complained. "This girl doesn't know how to clean or cook or understand when her presence isn't needed."

I wondered whether she ever washed her face. After a week or so it was clear that we would let her go at the end of the trial period. We hoped the girl wouldn't make a stink. Barbara had tried to train her and sympathized with her incompetence, but decided she would rather be her own maid than continue this way.

Barbara insisted that I be part of the firing squad. When told we were letting her go, the girl bowed her head as if she had experienced this before and knew it was coming. She said, "I learn," but packed her things in a shopping bag and left without objection.

We thought the girl was incompetent, but then we probably didn't even learn to pronounce her name right. We were as ignorant of her circumstances as she was of ours.

Barbara would not repeat the experience. "I don't need an amah to buy food or translate for me in the markets," she said. "I can point to what I want with precision. If the hawkers cheat it's not enough money to make a difference, far less than the cost of an amah." Besides, Barbara wasn't about to let anybody else determine what we would eat.

In time she would conclude that shopping with the amah was a ritual for many women in what was often a rather boring existence in a society of unemployed and inane wives of ambitious men. Barbara did not tell me at first, but the inane factor and the total preoccupation of the FSOs with their careers meant that neither she nor I made many friends among the consulate general families. She said, "I really like the Marlowes next door, but there's nobody else."

CHAPTER 8

Learning Cantonese

MY INTRODUCTION TO CANTONESE had started while I was still playing god with immigrant visa applications. Lung Sing, Mr. Rising Dragon in English, was charged with providing the 100 hours of language lessons offered to everyone at post. "We start by giving you a Chinese name," said Lung. "Goldsmith." Pause. "Chinese doesn't have the t-h sound." He mulled a bit. "Goldsmith. Gos-man for us. Gou Si-man." Gou Si-man it was, signifying tall, highly cultured. The name has stayed with me for more than fifty years.

My name was originally intended to sound as close to my English surname as a native Cantonese speaker could get. You would never know that if you heard it shouted in Mandarin or Taiwanese. Chinese dialects are as mutually incomprehensible as Finnish, Czech, and Greek. We learned that firsthand when Barbara's childhood friend, the pianist Lorin Hollander, came to perform and we took him out to dinner at a well-known restaurant on Paterson Street. At the table next to us were eight Chinese, all speaking English. Curiosity compelled me to go ask why they weren't speaking their own language. That brought a wave of laughter.

"Because English is the only language we all have in common," came the reply. "We come from different provinces and ended up here when Mao routed Chiang Kai-shek in the Civil War." The accent sounded like upper-class British.

Back in class, Lung Sing gave me a sheaf of papers with strings of letters that looked like the encrypted messages I had to decode during the Cuban Missile Crisis. "You won't get any Chinese characters now, because memorizing them would be so time consuming that you wouldn't learn to speak or understand much in your six months at New Asia College. We will study from Romanized materials, beginning with the basic sounds."

Lung wrote nonsense words on the blackboard: *guang, luo, faan, shih.* These were the Romanized versions of some basic sounds in Cantonese. Before I could begin to parse them I would have to learn how each of the letters was meant to be pronounced, alone, and together with each of its Roman alphabet neighbors.

"You should know," said Lung, "that we have fewer basic sounds than you do in English, but we more than make up for it with our tones. Some say we have nine different tones in Cantonese, but we teach the Yale system of seven tones. That is quite sufficient for foreigners to make themselves understood."

Lung explained that there is no agreement among linguists about the best way to Romanize Chinese sounds so foreigners can pronounce words correctly. "The Yale system is easier to use than Wade-Giles, which was developed in the nineteenth century. Then the Chinese communists could not stand for these foreign intrusions on their language, so we have their pinyin too. The three systems are like the Chinese dialects. If you learn to pronounce from one system, you will be hopelessly lost in another.

"Let's start. There are rising tones, falling tones, flat tones, sharp falling tones, high, low and middle. Try it. *Guang, guang, guang, guang, guang, guang, guang.* Seven distinct tones in all. All of them with different meanings in different combinations."

This galaxy of incomprehensible syllables rang in my head for two weeks before Lung Sing directed me to another sheet of paper with my first actual words in Cantonese. "My name is Gou Si-man. What is your name?"

Lung got me started for an hour a day during my adventures in Chinese efforts to get to their Gold Mountain in America. By January 1966 I had completed the basic 100-hour course and was let loose in the sea of Hong Kong humanity to commute across the harbor to the New Asia College total immersion program for missionaries.

On the Star Ferry I discovered the joy of studying a language my Mandarin-speaking colleagues considered a waste of time. For the proud China watchers, Cantonese was nothing more than a local dialect in a backwater colony. But for people native to the region, the real Chinese was Cantonese, not Mandarin.

The trip to Hung Hom was no more than twenty minutes, but it was perfect for mumbling newly acquired Cantonese vocabulary. I had my sheets of pattern sentences. The best way to transform those Romanized words to real language was to repeat them over and over, like a baby learns to speak.

Fellow passengers seated on either side of me quickly realized that I was trying to say something in their language. They gawked at this foreigner for only a moment before stepping in to help. In the beginning, I could say that I was an American. If I got that right, I said I was going to school, rather than to the bathroom or the railway station. Soon I was going shopping, to a movie, and all over town by repeating the "I am going" pattern more times than I could count.

I was reluctant to reveal to these kind helpers that I worked at the American Consulate General. It was not because I feared anti-Americanism. It was to avoid a lot of questions about how to get a visa to the US. I didn't want to claim that I was a missionary studying Chinese either. The Chinese regarded them very ambiguously, helpful to the poor, but all too eager to notch conversions on the pillars of their church beliefs. Since I was still a newly minted diplomat who had yet to master the art of prevarication, I usually revealed that I was an American Foreign Service Officer. Only a few of the ferry passengers who volunteered help asked about visas.

Most of my instant ferry friends said they had never seen a foreigner try to learn Cantonese. The colonial and expatriate attitude was why bother. Everybody knew that ambitious Chinese in the colony learned English as the path to opportunity. The only way they could communicate with the *faan gwai lo* was in the foreigners' tongue.

Passengers at my side often expressed delight at teaching me their language during those daily crossings of the most beautiful harbor in the world. And then we debarked into our separate lives, rarely finding ourselves together on the ferry again.

At New Asia College, it became clearer than ever that words are mastered after hearing them spoken hundreds or thousands of times. Starting as I did at the age of twenty-seven, this process had to be artificially created. "Repeat after me." One-on-one in six hours of classes every weekday. A new teacher every hour, six different teachers every day teaching another student each hour and looking like they enjoyed it.

These teachers were fully engaged with students who started out inchoate. Undoubtedly they were highly educated, but their work offered precious little opportunity to show it. Their instructions were to speak no English, unless it was otherwise impossible to explain the meaning or usage of the phrases they were trying to teach. I wondered how they managed to get through their simple sentence workdays in good cheer, repeating the same pattern sentences over and over again for each student, listening to language babies struggling with those tones all day long.

During breaks between classes I became acquainted with some of the missionaries who were also studying there. Language ability was essential for spreading the gospel. Though I was allergic to the concept of proselytization, I could not help but identify with my fellow pilgrims on our journey to holiness in Cantonese study. Most memorable was Father Ron Saucci, a gregarious, compelling, movie-star handsome guy of about thirty who would lead anybody to question why he ever went into the priesthood.

My incredulity was right on the mark. Ron told me that he also wondered how this ever happened. "My Italian immigrant family thought I was nuts. After the army in Germany I just couldn't settle down. A friend led me to the Maryknoll Fathers and everything happened from there. It was my best opportunity to be of service, and I desperately needed a purpose."

Ron was soon to work in a poor parish of refugees, starting a bakery with six employees that produced more than 5,000 buns a day for schools. Much of this nourishment went to the hungry mouths of children from the hillside squatter shacks who were Buddhist, Daoist, or worshippers of their ancestral gods. I doubt that Ron ever gave a thought to whether any of them might convert.

Ron and I and the other missionaries shared a desire to serve, but our education in Cantonese was quite different. They were learning to speak of their Lord. That was not why the Foreign Service sent me to study the language.

My need to speak of visas, US policy, and local political and economic issues made me an item of some curiosity and challenge to the teachers. The curriculum focused on the needs of the missionaries. There were no published teaching materials appropriate to the task of educating me. Once beyond polite talk and basic needs, we were in uncharted territory. My teachers had to make up vocabulary lists and grammar exercises on the spot. They were extraordinary in getting me to the language that I would need on the job.

No matter how fast the teachers said I was progressing, there was little of interest that I could actually express in Cantonese at the beginning. I was determined to learn faster, by intruding on the lives of strangers. The road from New Asia College to the ferry terminal was lined with small shops selling everything from calligraphy brushes to paint-ings and antiques, daily necessities and sweets. I would peer into these cubbyhole establishments with their musty odors and open doors in the rear that offered a view of a cramped corridor that was space for inventory, cooking and sleeping. Looking for somebody to practice my language on.

The proprietor and the staff usually were one and the same person waiting in the dim light for clients. Perhaps the foreigner coming into the store and asking "How is business today?" was a novel substitute for boredom. Sur-prised merchants were unfailingly patient as I tried to make sensible sentences and they tried to find simple terms to explain their trades. Sometimes I was treated to a history of a business started by a grandfather. Others told of flight from China with a few family treasures that became a shop selling old scrolls and antiques.

I prolonged these conversations, becoming fluent in, "How do you say this?" as I pointed to items for sale. Storeowners smiled and told me how well I was pronounc-ing my new vocabulary. Always polite, not always truthful. They let me try on my new language, and I wouldn't head for home until I had more than exhausted my command of it.

In those days long before cellphones, that meant that my wife Barbara never knew when I would get home, even though I tried to make it by dinner time. Although some of these shops did have phones, I didn't think to ask to call, nor did I understand that this was the height of incon-sideration. I was too engrossed in tongues.

Sometimes dinner would be cold. I knew enough not to complain, and Barbara didn't either. I'm afraid my inquiries into how her day went and her responses were perfunctory. I assumed she might have gone to the market, or window-shopping at Lane Crawford's, the luxury department store on Queen's Road Central. She learned a few phrases in Cantonese, but said that did not help her much. She enjoyed taking Shu-shu out for walks.

I had no real understanding of how she felt, or whether she shared any of my love affair with everything Hong Kong. Drunk with Cantonese, I went to my language classes oblivious to the trials of a consulate wife set adrift in a foreign culture and its incomprehensible language. I should have insisted that she be allowed to attend classes with me at New Asia College, but I was told that the State Department would say that was not possible, lathering budget constraints with a dollop of bureaucratic sympathy.

"Graduation" after six months was tinged with the regret of leaving behind a task that never could be finished. I had put my heart into a lot of talk; going, doing, comparing, and preferring in pattern sentences until I could do it on my own. The teachers would lose yet another student who had just arrived at the cusp of intelligent conversation, only to face another beginner again, while I would speak in Cantonese with people yearning to get to America, in the American Consulate General on Garden Road.

CHAPTER 9

Hal Christie's Parting Gifts

"WELCOME BACK. You're just in time for the summer visa rush." That was Hal Christie bringing me back into the visa section and briefing me on the Non-Immigrant Visa Unit, which processed all the tourist, business and student visas. Hal would soon depart Hong Kong, but not before he left me with two gifts. The first was a steady stream of introductions to musicians who would keep the coals of my passion glowing.

Moya Rea was a New Zealander, about fifty, elegant, dignified, and friendly, who struck me as timeless in appearance, always impeccable. She had come to Hong Kong with her husband in 1951. He was in charge of the Taikoo Dockyard, the largest in the colony. They lived in a mansion on a hilltop above Quarry Bay, built along with the shipyard by a *taipan* featured in Clavell's *Noble House*.

"Moya is Hong Kong's foremost accompanist and vocal coach," said Hal. "She's at the center of the classical music world here." I would learn from Nancy Zi that the Urban Council and Radio Hong Kong frequently went to her for recommendations and advice on performers to feature in their concerts and broadcasts.

Moya introduced me to other musicians, among them Lucy Gomersall, a Chinese widow with a somewhat small but very sweet soprano voice to match her petite stature and amiable disposition. She suggested that I do some obbligato accompaniments for Lucy in an upcoming concert. I was as happy with the offer as the *Lo, Hear the Gentle Lark* that she would sing. Moya also offered to be my pianist for the Poulenc sonata and the premier of composer Doming Lam's new work, *Wai City Ballad*.

I hoped we would perform before Hal left so I could tell him the concert was in his honor. He had bequeathed me a life in music in Hong Kong and shared his enthusiasm for the Foreign Service, a source of prestige and stable income that most musicians could not even dream about.

Hal's second gift was an insistent recommendation. "Take a few days off and celebrate graduation from language school before you get started in the visa mill. You and Barbara must visit Macau and savor the glory of the Bela Vista Hotel. By hydrofoil it takes about an hour. Forty miles and you'll feel like you're in a coastal town in Portugal."

We took Hal's advice and booked a morning hydrofoil that got us to Macau in time for lunch at the modestly elegant Portuguese-Macanese restaurant and sidewalk cafe by the Praia Grande, the bayside esplanade designed by and for the Portuguese. We had hardly been seated when two missionaries at the adjoining table invited us to their church and spoke of their hopes to establish the first college in Macau someday.

The seafood was excellent, flavors reminiscent of the meals I found in Mediterranean ports during my time in the navy.

The restaurant also featured sparkling wine that brought even more joy to our palates than French champagne.

Satiated, we checked into the Bela Vista and were treated by the host to a tour of the balustrade balconies that offered unparalleled views of the tiny colony and beyond. He pointed out the Chinese islands lining the route to Hong Kong and the tiny Macanese islets of Taipa and Coloane. Those specks of land were populated by fishermen and subsistence farmers who did everything in their rice paddies by hand. Never could we have imagined the huge gambling palaces that reside there now. Not that there wasn't plenty of gambling in Macau back then. Our host pointed out the Lisboa Hotel, the newest complex for gamers. "It's a big source of income so be careful."

Sensing that we wanted to get out and walk, he summed up quickly. "To the south and west you see the South China Sea and the rugged coast of Kwangtung province that almost hugs us. It's a land of poor farmers and fisherman. They bring their catch and their rice to market in tiny boats that aren't seaworthy in open water. You'll see them in the harbor."

We ambled down the hill from the hotel to the Praia Grande. The wide cobblestone promenade by the water was where the Portuguese and mixed-blood Macanese families paraded their eligible daughters to be observed on weekends. Elegant old houses across a tree-lined road appeared to be built from memories of Portugal. A short walk brought us to a restaurant famous for African chicken, operated by a transplant colonial who had served in Angola. At the tip of the peninsula stood a seventeenth-century fortress guarding against pirates and invaders.

In our wanderings we learned that you could easily walk the length of the peninsula from the fortress to the causeway leading into China in less than two hours, and across the center of the city from the Hong Kong–Macau ferry pier to the casino on the western waterfront in less than one. The city center featured squat rows of two- and three-story buildings housing goldsmith shops and small stores offering everything from necessities and cheap souvenirs for tourists to expensive antiques for serious collectors and fakes for suckers who didn't know the difference.

The highlight of our trip was a visit to the ruins of Saint Paul's Basilica, the most stunning historical relic of the first European settlement in the Far East. All that remained of this early seventeenth-century church after a fire in 1835 was the façade of cathedral magnificence, perched on top of a hill above a grand stairway leading to the entrance. The view of that imposing structure from the bottom of the stairway must have been planned to lead straight to heaven.

Back on earth, we came across a baboon caged into a wall enclosure by a small souvenir shop. Sympathetic to his plight in a space much too small, we stopped to have a look. The animal must have experienced many stares. He bared his teeth into a caricature of a smile, lifted his hand and masturbated. Thus began my fascination with Macau.

CHAPTER 10

The Tricks They Try

THOMINA THORESON WELCOMED ME into a small office partitioned off from the much larger immigrant visa section. There was a desk for each of us, along with a plain wooden chair for interviewees, no cushion.

Miss Thoreson clearly was my mother's generation but younger than sixty-two, since the Foreign Service imperative of worldwide availability had been codified into mandatory retirement at that age for all but ambassadors and special presidential appointees. She looked older than my mother, weathered with wrinkles and thinning hair gone completely gray. She smoked.

"Call me Tommie." After explaining that about fifteen minutes would be allowed for each visa interview, she showed me a 16x20 inch black and white framed picture. "This was the entire Washington staff in 1938. That's me and some 250 others on the front steps of the State Department with Secretary of State Cordell Hull."

I squinted at the picture that proved she was already in the service the year I was born. It certainly was her, recognizable and quite attractive. The revelation that the State Department was that small back then stunned me speechless. My orientation class for newly minted Foreign Service officers was told that we had approximately 3,000 officers and staff (FSO and FSS), plus some 6,000 civil service employees. The FSO and FSS corps served in our embassies and consulates overseas, as well as in Washington.

I knew that the government had expanded exponentially since World War II, but it was beyond my imagination to conceive of the department's entire Washington-based staff gathered on the front steps of that building. I studied the picture for a long time. We had more people than that in Hong Kong now.

Tommie had started out as a secretary, where most women staffers remained for the rest of their careers. She benefitted from opportunities provided by the wartime shortage of men. Eventually she was appointed as a consular officer, and in 1965 she was one of a very rare breed of Foreign Service women who were not FSS secretaries. The nickname Tommie chose fitted well in the almost exclusively men's world of FSOs. After a thirty-year career she now headed the non-immigrant visa section and had me and a local national employee who handled appointments and files as her assistants. She said this would be her retirement post. "I finally have some help, even if it's only for the summer rush."

We were both charged with independently determining whether visitor visa applicants would indeed be temporary visitors who had sufficient ties to Hong Kong to impel their return after a trip to the US. "Our responsibility is to make the correct determination based on the presumption of ineligibility," said Tommie. "The law requires us to know what's in their hearts. Then they have to show that they won't become public charges."

In Hong Kong and third-world countries the stipulations of US immigration law meant that visitor visas were only available to the wealthy. Student visas required either family wealth or talent so prodigious that a university offered a substantial scholarship.

Reading the minds of visa applicants was no mean task. Hong Kong's annual per capita gross domestic product was less than $700, far from enough to support a trip to the US, but there were plenty of applicants coming in with documents showing a substantial sum of money. Often it had been deposited in bank accounts established shortly before they came in for their appointments.

These applicants could show the money to pay for a trip, though sometimes it was just enough for a plane ticket. Our job was to ascertain where the money came from and determine the applicant's bona fides. I would have loved to have searched the abodes where all that cash was claimed to be stashed until just before the scheduled interview, but that was not in the job description.

For the elite, it was different story. The patriarchs of these very wealthy families told diplomats like me how they had placed their three sons: one in New York, one in London, and the third in Australia or Canada. They described their contingency plans for dealing with yet another Chinese upheaval. I don't think they ever could forget that Hong Kong's border with China was only an hour away, that the PRC claimed the colony as Chinese territory, and the British couldn't possibly defend it against a military takeover attempt.

We saw all kinds of visitor visa hopefuls aspiring to get to the Gold Mountain. Some presented urgent telegrams about critical business negotiations in the US, but no evidence of a business in Hong Kong. Beautiful young women well supported by sugar daddies commanded attention and sometimes enticed, but they faced disqualifying suspicion of prostitution. Students showed high scores on the standard Test of English as a Foreign Language (TOEFL), but could hardly say "I want go US." They couldn't explain the source of funds in the bank account established the day before, nor could they say anything about the university that accepted them or state where they took that TOEFL test. What were they thinking? How could they believe we would be so easily fooled?

In mid-June a twenty-three-year-old intending student from Macau handed me an impressive sheaf of papers along with his application. The information on his I-20 form provided by a well-known university in the Midwest documented acceptance in a graduate program in hydraulic engineering with a full tuition fellowship. His bank account showed regular deposits for several years, with sufficient funds to cover remaining expenses for at least a year. My local employee assistant perused the records he submitted and said they were for a family business that showed substantial income. The undergraduate transcripts from the university in Macau revealed a student with very high grades in every subject.

This certainly looked like a cut and dried case. High grades, a big scholarship, sufficient funds, and an acceptable TOEFL score. This Mr. Wong looked like a serious student. He wore thick glasses and appeared a bit awkward in a dark suit and tie. His demeanor was impeccable . . . impassive as he waited while I examined his documents.

I was tremendously impressed by Chinese students who had gotten this far in their studies. Most had gone through Hong Kong's British school system rather than the Cantonese-language schools, but they were still working in a second language. I could not have survived college education in Russian, French or any second language, much less Chinese. Most of all I was impressed by engineering students, because I had dropped out of pre-engineering at Columbia almost the minute I had to stand at a drawing board in the required sophomore graphics class.

This was an extraordinary application. It was no surprise that a student with a record like Mr. Wong's would be awarded a big scholarship at a university that wanted to add yet another country to its list of international students from all over the world. Most impressive of all was this applicant's ingenuity. And most unfortunate, because I was the designated vice consul accredited to Macau, and knew that there were no institutions of higher learning there, as our missionary friends who hoped to establish a college someday had told me.

I paused in my reading of the documents to look at the applicant sitting across from my desk. His face was expressionless as it had been since the beginning of the interview. He averted my gaze and stared at the window.

"You have a very thorough application here. Tell me about your college experience."

He hesitated. I waited.

He finally spoke. "I study very hard many years. Now I need continue in America to become engineer."

"This saddens me."

He twitched.

"This saddens me because your application is so well prepared that I know how badly you must want to study in the United States. *Hou chai chaam.* It's so sad because I also know there aren't any colleges in Macau."

It seemed as if his brow might touch his knees. He told me how he got the papers. The university's I-20 form gave every appearance of being authentic as he claimed. Everything else was fabricated: the transcripts, the TOEFL results, the business documents, even the long history of bank deposits which was rented rather than real.

I explained the law. "Fraud requires me to deny your application under provisions of the Immigration and Nationality Act that would render you ineligible for a US visa for life."

I watched his eyes sink to the floor. He had expended so much effort to win this graduate fellowship that I could not help but feel for him. Wong's gloom filled the room. I explained, "If you withdraw this application there will be no record of it and you can apply again someday. Otherwise I have no choice."

Eyes moist, Mr. Wong thanked me and made his way out of the office. Later that day Tommie Thoreson told me I did the decent thing. "It's no fun dashing people's dreams of getting to the Gold Mountain day after day."

Aside from a barely audible sigh before he left, I never heard from Mr. Wong again, but I have no doubt that he eventually devised a way to get to the US, legally or otherwise. He would have found a way to stay. After years of low wages he might have opened a small business and worked very hard to make it grow. I would bet on that, and would also bet that if he were fortunate enough to find a mate, his children and their children are likely to be among the best and brightest Americans today.

CHAPTER 11

Extravagant Invitations

LIFE IN NON-IMMIGRANT VISAS brought other surprises too. Invitations from the rich and famous. Quite a few of them. In the beginning I asked Tommie, "Why invite me?"

"Are you really surprised? Come on. If you made it into the Foreign Service you can figure this out."

"Well, I heard the section chiefs get invited by these people, but how did I get on their invitation list?" I was beginning to figure it out but Tommie interrupted before I could speak.

"It's a natural consequence of you sitting at that desk and playing god with everybody who comes in and asks for permission to go to the US."

It didn't take any brains to realize that these prominent people qualified for visas, though I had never seen any of them in the office. "But they have children and grand-children and other relatives who wouldn't qualify on their own if they came in cold to see us," said Tommie. "There's no way a ten-year-old could overcome the law's presumption that he's an intending immigrant, but our friends want to send that boy to a private school in California and

eventually get him a US passport. Think of the consequences for our relations here if we turn those kids down. You
get invitations from the *crème de la crème* to make sure that
neither we nor they lose face with a dumb refusal."

Tommie could not have been clearer. "You'll meet some
wonderful people. Wealthy beyond belief, kind to us peons,
and cultivated too. Enjoy those invitations, but be very
careful about people neither of us have ever heard of unless
our colleagues upstairs tell us it's important to see them.
Most of the others want us to overturn a previous rejection.
Sooner or later you'll be tempted with a bribe."

The fixed frown on Tommie's face told me she was dead
serious. I was quite relieved that she gave me the benefit of
the doubt and didn't come right out and say don't do it.

I accepted a lot of those invitations and proudly report
that I never accepted a bribe in my entire Foreign Service
career. We did reverse some negative visa decisions because
we should have. Law often demanded ridiculous rigidity
while diplomacy required reasonable good judgment. We
could not reject every student applicant because ninety
percent of those approved were known to change status
legally while in the US and become American citizens. We
could certainly play god, but the devils of regulation and
the angels of common sense were in constant conflict. We
had to resolve it.

Run Run Shaw, the movie and TV magnate, was everybody's favorite in the American Consulate General. He
regularly invited us to private showings of his films before
their public release. We learned to read the English subtitles
fast enough to keep up with the action. The Cantonese
dialogue burned my ears, but I took up the challenge to

understand what I could. After the show I felt amply rewarded for the effort by the petit fours and cordial hospitality. *The Sand Pebbles* was filmed partly in Hong Kong and we got to see a preview of Steve McQueen on screen too.

Run Run's generosity continued for a very long time. He donated nearly a billion dollars to charities, schools and hospitals in Hong Kong and Mainland China. One reward for his amiability and munificence was an unusually long life. He passed away in 2014, in his 107th year.

The Eu family hosted us in their medieval castle on a prime promontory near Victoria Peak. We approached the manor on a cobblestone walkway leading to towers and ramparts. Two complete suits of fifteenth-century armor stood guard at the entrance, with halberds and lances. I could not help but think that the traditional Chinese medicines, which brought the family an enormous fortune, might have been welcomed to salve the sore muscles from wearing that heavy armor.

One of the most extravagant invitations was to join C.Y. Tung for a daylong cruise on his *Seawise* in the waters surrounding Hong Kong. Tung was the founder in 1947 of the Overseas Orient Line. His 109-foot yacht was a five-star boutique hotel for the enjoyment of his guests. Servants in white livery serving drinks, canapés, and the lavish meal were so numerous that they responded to our desires before we could form them.

C.Y. introduced us to his son Chee-hwa, who became Hong Kong's first chief executive under Chinese rule in 1997 and was very unpopular. One of the most successful and flamboyant of the colony's crony capitalists, Tung the father gave us a glimpse of a lifestyle that Barbara and I would not have imagined had we not experienced a bit of it.

Among the most cultivated of this sampling of rich and famous hosts was the Chiu family. Yee-ha Chiu was a fine London-educated pianist introduced by Moya Rea to be my partner in an upcoming concert. We rehearsed in her home. Her father seemed fidgety with this intruder in his house of treasure, even though Yee-ha introduced me as an American diplomat. Mr. Chiu tested my Cantonese and appraised me very carefully before showing me a collection of Shang dynasty bronzes that would have been the envy of museums. He squirmed when I asked how he acquired it and brought the bronzes out of China. "Family heirlooms. Make music for me." I dared not question him further.

It was only at a later rehearsal without her father present that Yee-ha explained. "The great British trading houses like Jardine Matheson relied on compradors who served as their middle men in trade with China. Some of today's great wealthy families made their fortunes as compradors in the nineteenth-century opium trade. My father will never speak of that."

Barbara and I also savored a genuine friendship with a couple from a very different class of people. Morris and Sylvia Birnbaum had come to Hong Kong to manufacture fancy women's dresses with piecework seamstresses stitching high-value clothing for about a dollar a day. Like many early foreign investors in Hong Kong's cheap labor economy, they had done very well.

In a corner of the globe where American Jews were rare, friendship came surprisingly easy because we had been born in America into a tiny minority which had suffered so much persecution for so many centuries. Since I had been called a dirty Jew more than once as I grew up in Upper Montclair, N.J., I knew why Jews tended to feel comfortable with their own kind, less so in the Christian world in which we tried to make our way.

"We're intrigued by the smart Jewish boy who chooses public service when you could be making a lot of money too." They said so. It was corollary to that earlier question, "Why would a nice Jewish boy want to go into the Foreign Service?" We said how glad we were to have friends who didn't care how little money we made. We got along famously, riding together in their convertible to the Clearwater Bay Marina to share stories on their forty-six-foot yacht as we plied Hong Kong's island-studded waters.

And there were the simple pleasures Barbara and I shared alone, a good meal and a stroll in the neon jungle of the Kowloon Peninsula, a mini-concert of traditional Chinese music on a sampan in the Causeway Bay typhoon shelter, a ride on the top deck of the trolley until we picked an intriguing spot to get off and look around the real Chinese Hong Kong.

By that standard the four-year-old Chevy Bel Air I bought from my fastidious math teacher for $875 marked us clearly as upper class. We drove leisurely and discovered Big Wave Bay on the southeast corner of Hong Kong Island. Bus service was all but nonexistent. The locals couldn't afford a taxi. For us it became a symbol of special privilege for the colonials and expats. We white people had the sheltered bay and its glorious waves to ourselves. That's where Barbara told me she was pregnant.

CHAPTER 12

Kam-lan

I GAVE BARBARA SUCH A BIG HUG that she might have feared for the baby. Love and pride at this affirmation of my manhood.

Six months had passed without an amah and I was convinced that there really was no need. "That's true," said Barbara, "but we're invited out often enough that we're going to need a babysitter, and I want plenty of time to train one that I can trust."

We had learned that amahs had long been a fixture in Hong Kong. Upscale apartment complexes were designed to house live-in amahs inconspicuously in lowest floor cubicles about the size of the bathrooms upstairs. This avoided the inconvenience of sharing living space with the help while keeping the amahs at the beck and call of their masters.

Amahs earned little by our standards, but the going wage of fifty dollars a month for one who knew enough English to work for expatriates placed these domestics solidly in the middle class of Chinese workers. Many of them made a lifelong profession of it and remained single. They were well organized, dominated by women of long experience who valued their economic independence above all else.

Chinese friends said they saved voraciously and there were numerous associations of amahs who owned property, some of it rented to foreigners. Though they were servants in the home and disadvantaged in many ways, the professionals were savvy. They typically started at age eleven or twelve apprenticing to an older relative, and were still relatively young after twenty or thirty years of service when they became property shareholders and established themselves at the top of the domestic-labor hierarchy.

A neighbor's amah who looked to be forty or fifty promised to bring us a very good worker. When I answered the knock on our door that evening I was taken aback by a pretty girl who looked even younger than the pimply one we had let go earlier. She was not movie-star beautiful, but very attractive, animated, fresh, and nervous. She looked like a schoolgirl, hardly an applicant to be a domestic helper. I invited her in Cantonese to come in and sit on the living-room sofa.

She seemed quite startled and came in just far enough to squat on her haunches by the upholstered chair nearest our vestibule. "Please sit," I repeated, as surprised by her response as she must have been by my invitation. She did not move.

"We do not sit on the master's furniture. My name is Kam-lan and I want to work for you." She spoke barely above a whisper, in English. Again I invited her to sit. "Not our custom. I stay here." Her black trousers tightened at the knees and thighs as she continued to squat.

"Do you have any experience working as a maid?" Not possible, I thought. She couldn't be any older than fifteen or sixteen.

"Oh yes. Six years already."

Towering over her while she squatted felt even more awkward than the realization that I'm being asked to exploit child labor. That pretty young face looked up at me. How could she possibly have six years' work experience? But there was nothing in her expression to suggest that she was lying.

"I working with my aunt since I was eleven years old. She train me very well."

I didn't know how to respond, even though my own experience included more or less regular employment from the age of ten onward. I mowed lawns for my parents' friends for a dollar. Later there was a newspaper delivery route. Throughout high school it was twenty-three hours a week at J&L Meyers Five and Ten, three hours after school on weekdays and all day Saturday.

"We could not afford middle school," she said. "After primary school not free. No money for that." Then she blushed. "I was first in my class but I could not continue. Eight brothers and sisters in my family." While I spoke to her in Cantonese, she continued to respond in English. "I studied by myself. From comic books."

I was convinced that this teenager was unusually intelligent. "Would you be willing to help me with my Cantonese?"

She hesitated for a moment, as if that was crazy inappropriate to ask of a maidservant who should squat when seeking employment. "Yes. I try that and do good work too."

Up until this point Barbara had been busying herself in the kitchen. She knew that I wanted to interview in Cantonese, and had no trouble accepting my foibles, including a desire to be the first to interview the prospective servant that she would have to live with all day long. "But I'm not going to stand silent beside you while you chat up a woman in a language I don't speak."

Our agreement was that when I was satisfied with showing off my Cantonese and had formed an impression of the candidate, I would fetch her in the kitchen so she could conduct her own interview in English. Barbara came out and asked Kam-lan about her background and what tasks she would be willing and able to undertake.

"Anything you want, missy."

We took her on.

Not long afterwards I asked Kam-lan to join me on the sofa and help with some Cantonese sentence patterns. I wanted her to accept that it was not necessary to squat when I spoke with her.

"Not comfortable with that." It was more than a month before she came to understand that my "please sit" conveyed across our profoundly different cultures and stations in life did not mean she should ignore it and squat anyway.

Kam-lan worked on my pronunciation, corrected my grammar, and even taught me colloquial ways of saying things that I had learned only in the stiff formal language of the classroom at New Asia College.

As I practiced my Cantonese and Kam-lan realized I really was inviting her to sit on the sofa, I came to enjoy her company for its own sake. In bits and pieces she revealed herself, as much as she was willing to do while maintaining a safe and respectable distance between "master" and amah.

"I have little contact with my family in Pok Fu Lam Village after I leave to work with auntie." She had been eleven when amah's quarters replaced her home in the village. Childhood was over. The aunt trained her in everything that might be expected of an amah. "I learn to clean, shop, speak English, care for baby." Her employers never learned a word of Chinese. The most recent was an English couple that required breakfast to be prepared every day but Sunday. "I learn to do that too, poached eggs and kippers." Sunday normally was a day off when she went out for some amusement with her aunt. Often it was window-shopping items she could not dream of buying.

Kam-lan said her family used to be far from poor. "Grandfather was a successful dry-goods merchant before the Japanese took everything in the War. It broke his spirit. We had nothing." She said she learned this from the aunt who introduced her to the amah world when mother was overwhelmed with the care of eight children. "I was the third child, born in 1948."

Her father was a truck driver for Dairy Farm, the largest dealer in dairy products in Hong Kong. About his driving skills, Kam-lan could tell me nothing, but she was keenly aware of his proclivity for procreation. "Besides my mother's eight children, he had a child by a second woman. That one left him when she discovered he already had a wife. Now he has eight children by a third wife, so we never see him."

Kam-lan said her schooling was rigorous, leaving little time to play. After school she was saddled with helping her mother care for the succession of infants who came after her in rapid order. The older brother went off to work in a repair shop while a sister worked in a plastic-flower factory for a while and dropped out of sight. Lucky the aunt took her on as a helper, so she wasn't forced to work in one of those factories that mercilessly exploited labor.

I might excuse my ignorance of Kam-lan and Barbara's daily routine because I was too preoccupied with probing the hearts and minds of visa applicants whose aspirations of getting to the Gold Mountain were at the mercy of my decisions. A more accurate appraisal is that I wasn't really curious enough to retain what I was told. Barbara did say that Kam-lan quickly took over all of the housework and was intent on learning how to cook the way she did. It wasn't long before I couldn't distinguish who was doing the cooking on any given day.

CHAPTER 13

Political Apprentice

MY STINT IN VISAS WAS OVER. Don Ferguson welcomed me to the Economic Section for my next training assignment. He would get me started as apprentice Hong Kong/Macau political officer until his successor arrived in two weeks. Al Harding would take over and be my mentor for the next several months. Don said Al was the only other FSO who spoke Cantonese.

"Why would a lone political officer be placed in the Economic Section?" I asked.

Don explained, "Reporting on local political developments doesn't fit in with the China watchers in the Political Section. They're totally preoccupied with developments in the PRC. We're housed here in the Econ Section because Hong Kong politics are about economic policy and business influence. The general public has no voice in either." With that, Don took me into the section chief's office for the introduction.

Lynn Olson offered a limp handshake. He was tall and mostly bald, with strands of gray hair combed partly over his forehead. He seemed to be in his mid or late fifties and tired of it. Without even a hint of a smile, his welcome was

curt advice. "Comb the newspapers for items that might
be of interest and write them up for the 'Weeka.' That's the
summary every Friday of news that doesn't merit a separate
cable report. The position is also responsible for reporting
on Macau, but nothing ever happens there. Don will brief
you." He dismissed us and turned away.

Don gave me a quick introduction to his files. "This is
a good time to get familiar with them because I have to go
meet the movers." He half whispered, "Olson is nearing
mandatory retirement and teeming with resentment. His
contemporaries are running important operations and some
of them are ambassadors."

I had a week to catch Don Ferguson on the run with my
questions. He assured me that my short stint alone would
be a quiet one. "Nothing will happen over the coming
weeks. The Brits take long vacations and there hasn't been
a serious disturbance since the 1956 riots. Look at what's
happening over the border instead."

The big Hong Kong political news during the summer
of 1966 was the appearance of the "Little Red Book" of
Chairman Mao's quotations. The international community
scoffed at the latest manifestation of Mao personality cult,
but thought it would make a great souvenir for friends and
relatives back home. I bought a copy but never read it.
Pravda propaganda had been more than enough for me.

Many organizations in Hong Kong were loyal to the
Chinese communists. The heads of the New China News
Agency and the Bank of China were appointed by Peking.
Competing Nationalists aligned with the Kuomintang
government that lost the Civil War and fled to Taiwan also
boasted a network of organizations in the colony. There

were Chinese Communist and Taiwan Nationalist supported unions, bookstores, emporiums and civic associations living side by side under the protection of the colonial government.

The British carefully monitored political activity and effectively suppressed conflict originating from either side. "The Nationalist groups are viewed as a pain in the neck," said Don, "but the key point is that the communists aren't making trouble. That's because the British stake in keeping Hong Kong tranquil matches Chicom interests. This is China's window on the West. Trade with and through Hong Kong accounts for half of PRC foreign currency reserves. They're not going to kill the goose that lays the golden egg." Don's assessment was two months before Mao welcomed millions of Red Guards in Tiananmen Square on August 18, 1966 and urged perpetual revolution.

With that swan song from Don Ferguson, I was left alone in my cubicle with my unopened copy of Mao's Little Red Book and responsibility for reporting the politics of a colonial regime that suppressed politics. I thought that anybody in the only Hong Kong political officer position would feel lonely in a mission larger than most embassies. The building was swarming with China watchers from numerous agencies claiming part of the action, but I didn't know anybody who gave a hoot about the politics of appointed colonial councils. No wonder Don Ferguson was anxious to leave and get on with his life.

It was also a no-brainer to see that Mr. Olson was preoccupied and I was just another bump on his log. I spent much of that summer waiting for Al Harding and further guidance. Neither came.

CHAPTER 14

My First Chinese Wedding

OF COURSE THERE WAS NO WAY I could find all the tidbits fit to print in the Weeka on my own. Don Ferguson told me that the juiciest morsels to share with the folks in Washington would be in the Chinese-language press, but I was *man mahng*—illiterate. I could only read a few Chinese characters and I was still putting all my effort into the spoken language.

I shouldn't have been ashamed. Nearly all of the FSOs were heavily dependent on locally hired Chinese assistants. The Administrative Section officers relied on locals for assistance with every process from employees' arrival to their departure: check-in, housing, move-in, move out, shipping household effects and more. The visa section could not function without local employees to examine Chinese documentation, translate interviews, and manage applicant files. Political and economic officers also relied on their local assistants. Although the China watchers could read Chinese, few Americans trained as adults could dream of parsing those ideographs anywhere near as fast as an educated Chinese who grew up with the language. It was far less costly to have the local nationals do the initial reading of Chinese materials and prepare summary translations for the FSOs, who would call for the original texts of items they thought important.

Thomas Hui was my indispensable assistant. He read the Chinese papers for me and made it his mission to ensure that I understood the complexities of an overwhelmingly Chinese place where government was totally controlled by British colonials and their appointees.

He was in his early thirties, a few years older than I and about three inches shorter, but his five feet five inches was at least average height in a population that had known hunger and chaos much of their lives. His pitch-black hair was showing strands of gray. I thought early malnutrition and turned out to be right, but he was normal weight now.

Thomas told me that his boyhood was spent fleeing the communists during the civil war. "I became an expert at pressing myself flat against the roof of railroad cars so I wouldn't be decapitated in tunnels. Sometimes I had no choice but jump off and wait for another opportunity to get as far away from the fighting as I could. I had to beg for food or steal it."

Thomas was unfailingly polite. Many of the Chinese I met were almost ritually polite. I asked him about that.

"You get polite talk because Chinese will not say no, or reveal their intentions, or how they feel about you. Most of us feel that you have all the power and we have none."

Such irony, I thought. Thomas had almost absolute power to determine what I would learn from the Chinese press. He would bring me summary translations of selected items every day and I would ask him what the deeper implications were of what I read in English.

Thomas invited me to his wedding banquet a few weeks after we started working together. The invitation said 6:30 p.m., but "You are an honored guest and don't need to arrive until at least seven." Nor was I expected to bring the customary *lai see,* the red envelope with a cash wedding present. Thomas explained: "Foreign guests are not expected to meet Chinese obligations."

Red envelopes. How practical, I thought. Guests are expected to give at least enough to cover the cost of their dinner, hopefully more. That would help defray expenses so great that weddings were often delayed for years to save money for all the obligatory celebrations. Close relatives gave more if they could. So did people who had a lot of money and wanted to show it.

I knew almost nothing of wedding customs and little of Thomas' background beyond his harrowing tales of escape. He was educated, dedicated to his middle-class job, and doing well enough by his early thirties to afford to marry a woman I never saw again after the wedding. The advice that I shouldn't arrive until a half hour or more after invitation time was his idea of good manners. Perhaps it was also meant to establish my status and spare me the small talk with people I had never met.

I arrived promptly at 7 p.m. to a cacophony of chattering guests who filled the banquet hall. In front of a sea of curious stares I was led to an empty seat at a table of strangers who felt no need to introduce themselves. We might call it rude. They probably assumed I wouldn't understand a word of it, so why waste? If Thomas' real intent was to have all the guests witness the arrival of a so-called important white-skinned official, he succeeded admirably.

When I regained my composure I assumed my Chinese identity and introduced myself as the "humble name" Gou, "big name" Si-man. There was a moment of shock at my table, but the guests recovered so quickly that you would miss it if you didn't know. "You speak such wonderful Chinese," came the standard opening to foreigners who attempted a simple greeting. Even today, if you learn how to do a hatchet job on *m'goi,* you will be regaled with praise for your linguistic ability. No matter that "thank you" is the only thing you could say and your *m'goi* was in the wrong tone.

I did my best to make conversation during the twelve-course banquet, telling my tablemates where I came from and how long I studied Cantonese. "Oh, you're such a brilliant student." With more banquets I learned that speaking Cantonese transformed me into a performing monkey. I wanted to say that, but it would have been taken as gross though true. Instead, "I'm just a poor student who learned only a hair on the skin." "Thank you for the compliment" would have been pride or arrogance. Polite talk was a challenge, all through dinner.

At the very end of the banquet I was peeling an orange and preparing to enjoy that follow-on to a gummy sweet red-bean cake dessert when the other eleven guests at the table stood up as one and made for the door without a word.

So much for my understanding of Chinese weddings. Only after I sat stunned for a while did I begin to sense that maybe the time for socialization at weddings was before the meal, not afterwards. Too late for the occasion, Thomas confirmed that once the last dish was served the guests were expected to get up and leave, accepting the offer of hard candy and a cigarette from the newlyweds on the way out.

CHAPTER 15

Leisure Time

THERE WAS AMPLE TIME for recreation during this period that I was scavenging for the Weeka. FSOs were offered complimentary use of the Hong Kong Cricket Club, which was just a few minutes' walk down the hill from the consulate general. The tennis courts by the cricket pitch were grass like at Wimbledon, providing the perfect venue for my resounding defeat in the second round of the 1966 Hong Kong Open.

I commiserated with Barbara that the Ladies Recreation Club made no such offer to the consulate general wives. "Never mind," she said. "You know I'm not a club person anyway." Rather strange, I thought, since she grew up on a resort where her father was a manager.

At home I played flute to my heart's content, perhaps causing Barbara to wish that she was at a club after all. But she never said so.

The next concert would be a performance with Nancy Zi. She was a soprano with a powerful and lilting voice and great musical taste. She was also quite unlike the divas who dominated opera houses all over the Western world. Slim and svelte, relatively tall, Nancy didn't look anything at all like the typical Brünnhilde of *Der Ring des Nibelungen*. She was concrete evidence that it was not necessary to be heavy to have a big voice. Though we did not have a lot of rehearsal time together, our performance in the City Hall Concert Hall went really well. We grasped hands tightly and promised to do another one in the midst of the applause.

Afterwards a man about my size and age came up with words of praise and introduced himself as the bandmaster of The Queen's Own Buffs, a British regiment assigned to the Hong Kong Garrison. "I'm Stuart Macintyre. Also a flutist. When can we play duets together?"

My first thought was why would any real flutist want to play in a band? My distaste for high-school bands that made nothing but noise ran deep. I must have been uppity about guarding my self-appointed role as *the* flutist in the Hong Kong musical firmament. I tried to fend off the invitation, but Stuart persisted in his proposal, and I agreed to a date with something less than great enthusiasm.

Somewhat to my surprise, he and his wife Pauline and Barbara and I became the closest of friends, still in touch fifty years later. We got together socially and made music often, though we never took to the concert stage together. "That is a matter of social class," said Stuart. "The regimental commander would never permit a mere sergeant to do such a thing with a diplomat."

We invited Stuart and Pauline to dinner and asked them whether they might be willing to take care of Shu-shu for a few days while we went to Japan on vacation. They said, "Just fine." Shu-shu seemed fine with it too. He had already licked their hands when they visited before.

One day Stuart took Shu-shu and his son out for a walk and it wasn't just fine any more. As they were leaving their regiment's residential compound the old gate came crashing down on Shu-shu's head. He was in a coma several days, and was still paralyzed when we returned to pick him up. The Macintyres couldn't bear to put him down. Shu-shu looked at us plaintively, as if wondering why he couldn't move to lick us welcome. We couldn't bear to put him down either.

Barbara insisted that we take him home. I wasn't about to disagree. Shu-shu was such a nice dog before the accident. Our baby from before we expected another. Barbara was a nurse before she married me. She hung a sling from the ceiling, cradled Shu-shu in it and moved his legs up and down for days and weeks until he could stand. I did a little bit, but Kam-lan told me that Barbara was giving Shu-shu intensive care all day long. Eventually he could walk, after a fashion, but he had other problems. He was blind in one eye, and he walked only in circles. The brain damage was beyond recovery, but he still licked our hands. Barbara had saved the patient. Shu-shu would spend far more time with her than I could. Her bond with Shu-shu was as poignant as it was intimate.

Within a year, Stuart was transferred out of Hong Kong on short notice. It was only twenty years later when I visited him in London that he told me he had been sent back to England long before the end of his assigned tour of duty, guilty of intruding on someone of much higher social class: me.

That helps me understand why I was never offered access to government officials other than Emrys Davies, the reserved but helpful Foreign and Colonial Office's assistant political advisor to Governor Sir David Trench. One of Emrys' tasks was to deal with people like me. Everybody has his place in British colonial society.

After one of our rehearsals Nancy Zi told me about her uncle Ma Si-cong, who had stayed on in China after Mao took power. He was the founder and head of the National Music Conservatory in Beijing. That leading institution for Western classical music in China had been targeted by Red Guards as a center of bourgeois decadence.

She recounted the horror her uncle had been through in a torrent of words: "He was targeted in big-character posters and demonstrations outside the conservatory. They paraded him through the streets in a dunce cap and forced him to face snarling mobs screaming epithets denouncing him as a counter-revolutionary. The mob flailed him with posters cursing him as bourgeois. He lost the will to live. That's how Red Guards honored him for his dedication to music education.

"Those Red Guards are on a rampage everywhere. Everybody lives in fear." With that, Nancy quickly regained her composure. And I had my first taste of the sadness seeping into lives here in Hong Kong from the Cultural Revolution maelstrom in China.

I shared her story with a friendly freckle-faced China watcher from the Political Section, Burt Levin. He was thirty-six at the time and had already made a name for himself and offended some with a think piece predicting that the Vietcong would eventually outlast us in Vietnam because Americans would tire of paying the horrible cost of continuing the fight.

Burt reminded me that idealists who had devoted their lives to the Communist Party were being dismissed and sent to the countryside for "re-education" in droves. Thomas Hui had already told me that a lot of horror stories were coming out of the Mainland, often as messages making their way to relatives who had sought refuge in Hong Kong years before. "Another in the litany of sad tales coming out of China these days," said Burt.

The gruesome tales didn't stop Barbara and I from enjoying our free time and the company of the Birnbaums on their yacht and the Macintyres in our home. Stuart and I played duets while our wives gabbed and cooked. Barbara's pregnancy was a happy one. There was a certain solace watching Shu-shu make his way in circles as we strolled on Coombe Road to Wan Chai Gap Park.

Thomas Hui was a huge contributor to my education, and not just in the office. He introduced me to a group of friends who enjoyed weekend hikes along Hong Kong's numerous trails. Getting away from the city crowds was easy. Most stops along the Kowloon-Canton railway were only a few minutes' walk from trails that led to lush semi-tropical countryside and the rugged interior of the New Territories. Buses stopped by trailheads on Hong Kong Island that led to ridges offering views of sparkling waters out to nearby islands and the South China Sea. Spectacular cityscape and shoreline panoramas awaited those who climbed the colony's many steep hills.

In the far northeastern corner of the New Territories, trails led through paddy land and villages populated by Hakka people. I was surprised to see that only women worked the fields. Old men and young children hung around their homes and played on the dirt roads in the villages. One of my hiking companions explained: "The working-age men are in England. They take jobs in restaurants or as laborers. They'll stay for years before coming back for a short visit. The ones who saved their money built those newer houses. Then they go back to England to work again."

Meanwhile, the women worked tirelessly in the rice paddies to feed their children and their parents, without much surplus to sell.

We hiked trails that had been traditional routes between villages for centuries. When I greeted two women on a steep narrow stretch leading from Sha Tin into hill country they stared in shock. *"Faan gwai lo* speaks Cantonese." My surprise was to see such slightly built women in pajamas carrying heavily laden baskets balanced precariously on the ends of bamboo poles slung over their shoulders. Hard to believe that they depended on such ancient transport so close to the modern city. I asked, "Why this steep hilly route?"

One of the women was still staring. The other said, "This is the way home. The only way." She showed me a blue woman's jacket. "We get the clothes from the factory and bead and sequin at home. Factory pays by the piece. Much better than working there."

When we stopped at a tiny shop for beer after the hike my companions elaborated. "In the factory it would be ten hours a day of squalor. Labor laws are a sick joke. The government doesn't give a damn and couldn't do much if they did." They explained that the power of labor unions was limited by the small scale of manufacturing and the desperate need of most workers to hold on to a job and the meager income it provided, often less than a dollar a day.

Replacements for the lower-skilled workers who were the mainstay of Hong Kong's economy were easy to find and train. When it came to hiring and firing or settlement of disputes, the balance was overwhelmingly in management's favor. Some of my hiking friends opined that there was real trouble just below Hong Kong's appearance of calm. There had been two days of riots over a proposed raise in Star Ferry first-class fares that spring when I was in language school and unaware of anything but elementary Cantonese. "Another eruption is just a matter of time."

Thomas Hui countered that thought. "It's possible, but people fled to Hong Kong to get away from trouble, not cause it."

CHAPTER 16

Tidbits

B Y MID-AUTUMN OF 1966 the Cultural Revolution was producing perpetual Red Guard struggles and purges in Peking. President Liu Shaoqi, Deng Xiaoping, and other leaders were branded as bourgeois reactionaries and capitalist roaders. Nancy Zi's famous uncle Ma Si-cong was in re-education camp. His wife and children were in hiding and the family's property was seized by Red Guards.

Throughout all the turmoil Hong Kong remained calm. Al Harding did not arrive to take up his Hong Kong/ Macau political officer assignment.

There was no news when he would. He and his Danish wife were believed to be somewhere in Scandinavia on vacation, but nobody knew where they were or why he hadn't arrived by Labor Day as expected. I wasn't aware of what efforts might have been made to contact him, but they weren't successful.

Evidently Harding wasn't in any hurry to get to Hong Kong. Like many FSOs he probably had forgone a lot of home leave at the request of supervisors and was determined to use what he earned rather than forfeit it without any compensation. I heard a rumor that when he used up all his leave he would take early retirement.

I had the job to myself, with very little supervision from Mr. Olson of sour fatigue. Sometimes I wondered how the very experienced officers assigned to this position could consider the job challenging, but for me it was a great opportunity to learn about Hong Kong and the workings of the consulate general.

We were a huge mission, larger than most embassies. Besides the consul general and his deputy, we had five China watchers in the Political Section and five more FSOs in the Economic Section. The Consular Section occupied the whole second floor of our building on Garden Road, while the United States Information Agency boasted a senior public affairs officer and information, press, and cultural officers. There was a commercial officer, but no labor officer. The military was represented by army, navy and air force liaison officers with their assistants. Justice (FBI) and science liaison officers also were assigned to Hong Kong. Numerous local national assistants served the various sections and a large administrative staff supported everybody. Then there was a sizeable marine guard detachment responsible for physical security, with a guard always at attention at the lobby entrance. The most personable marine was Lance Corporal Heffernan, whose sister Cathy married Supreme Court Justice William O. Douglas that summer. The last of his four wives, she was twenty-two and he was sixty-seven, bringing national attention to the couple and local curiosity to the amiable corporal.

The building on Garden Road hosted more than 200 employees, but I can't say how many because I never learned the size of the CIA contingent. Along with the China watchers in the Political Section, those operatives in the shadows were the stars in the firmament. Hong Kong was the US window on China, and following developments there was the top priority.

Mr. Olson said there was plenty of information available about China, but the political officers knew precious little about what was really going on in Peking. Much less could they determine who was in control in the rest of the country. He gave the impression of being jealous of their exalted status in the mission. I was quite content to call the Hong Kong/Macau Political Section mine, for the moment.

CHAPTER 17

Richard Nixon, CODEL

I WAS INTRODUCED to the world of Congressional Delegations and soon enough I would learn that news of a forthcoming CODEL was met with muttered curses from the mouths of designated control officers.

Congressmen traveled often, and they loved to visit desirable corners of the earth where the link to their responsibilities was tenuous. Frequent questionable junkets at taxpayer expense were roundly criticized, but nobody seemed able to stop them.

President Johnson was getting us increasingly involved in Vietnam. Voter concern and policy interests gave many of our senators and representatives reason to seek firsthand reports. On many of these trips our elected representatives brought their wives along and spent more time in the British colony than in Vietnam. We developed a keen awareness of congressional shopping habits, because our distinguished guests asked our advice and assistance in getting the best of whatever they desired: cameras, jewelry, clothing, even furniture. Sometimes we were asked to bargain for them.

Since it was imperative to keep our senators and congressmen happy, control officer responsibilities were tasked to mid- and senior-level officers. These included arranging the schedule in every detail before the CODEL took off from Washington, meeting at the airport, appointments, logistics, entertainment, and dealing with any request that might be made during the course of the visit. Junior officers like me were called upon to handle bits and pieces until we were considered ready to take on a CODEL on our own.

Consul General Rice normally went to the airport to meet VIPs, for a very good reason. If you aspired to be an ambassador or assistant secretary of state it was essential to cultivate these people. High-level appointments were and are subject to a great deal of politicking and to Senate approval.

CODEL interest in more than just briefings stayed with me throughout my Foreign Service career. Later, in Taipei, one notably boorish congressman was quite open about his desire for sex, and I felt pretty sure he was expecting me to pay for it. Fortunately, our good friends in the Nationalist Party (KMT) knew where their interests lay.

I called our special contact in KMT headquarters. "Bring the honored guest to Peitou this evening," he said. "We'll take care of everything. You too." Because this congressman was so rude and crude, it didn't take much to convince that KMT official to ask the puzzled mama-san to provide him the ugliest prostitute she could find.

We were pleased with the selection, who looked more like a scullery worker than an entertainer. In the only display of manners I saw during the congressman's visit, he accepted the offering, unaware that custom allowed for rejection until the client was satisfied with the proffered partner.

During my service in Hong Kong there were also memorable CODEL moments. In November 1966, I was called up to the front office by the deputy chief of mission, Allen Whiting. He asked me to escort Richard Nixon to the car that would take him to his next appointment. Six years after his loss to Kennedy, Nixon was preparing another run for the presidency.

He did not offer his hand when we were introduced. As we walked down the stairs together, the future president asked, "What's your favorite football team?"

"Montclair High School. I never saw us lose a game. We were state champions every year but one."

"I meant college team."

"I never saw my Columbia College team win a game. We were the laughing stock of the Ivy League." I saw what might have been a wan smile. Evidently preoccupied, Nixon got in the car without another word and left.

There was already shock in the consulate general about the visit. Many of us knew that Consul General Rice did not go to the airport to meet Nixon. We were aware that Nixon had been a McCarthyite and a notorious pursuer of imagined traitors while serving on the House Un-American Activities Committee. He was the most prominent among the witch-hunters blamed for the totally unjustified purge of the most capable China hands in the Foreign Service. These FSOs had reported accurately what they saw of Mao Tse-tung's capabilities in Yunnan during WWII and recommended maintaining contact with the likely winners of China's Civil War. Their reward for deep understanding was accusations of disloyalty and blame for losing China to the communists. Five of these China experts, John Stuart Service, John Paton Davies, John Emmerson, John Carter Vincent, and O. Edmund Clubb, were publicly disgraced and forced to resign. Only decades later were they exonerated and honored by the State Department they had served so loyally.

Edward Earl Rice had served in China from 1935 until 1945, and barely survived the purge. He and many others in the Foreign Service detested Nixon. There is ample evidence that the enmity was mutual, including a report that then President Nixon told Kissinger on November 13, 1972 that he was determined that his "one legacy is to ruin the Foreign Service." This according to a January 4, 2007 *Washington Post* report on newly released State Department documents.

We gossipers in the consulate general were pretty sure that the boss had refused to see Nixon at all during that visit. It's hard to believe that Mr. Rice would not have known that Nixon was never one to forget a slight. His career was quickly over when Nixon became president.

Another aspect of that Nixon visit did not come to light until a few years after my CODEL experience in Taipei, and it has been a subject of speculation ever since. A *People* magazine article dated October 4, 1976 claimed that Nixon met a cocktail waitress named Marianna Liu in the Hilton Hotel lounge during his 1966 visit and she visited him in his room. Ms. Liu, who had moved to Nixon's home town of Whittier, California and worked as a domestic, was suing the *National Enquirer* over two stories that August "which said that she and Nixon had carried on a 'hot and heavy' romance," that she had seen him at the White House after he became president and that the FBI suspected her of being a communist spy. Ms. Liu's lawyer reportedly said Nixon was so angry about the accusations that he volunteered to testify on her behalf.

A 1976 *New York Times* report asserted that the FBI had investigated Nixon's relationship with Liu. The intelligence community was worried that Nixon could have spilled state secrets. The rumors persisted for decades. A February 4, 2005 article appearing in the *South China Morning Post* referred to rumors that the affair dated back to 1958 when Nixon visited Hong Kong while he was vice president.

I had no idea. During my few minutes with the man who was to become president, Nixon struck me as cold, too distant and stand-offish to strike up a real conversation or a casual affair. I can only state that all we talked about during that brief encounter in 1966 was football.

CHAPTER 18

Hong Kong Non-Politics

THROUGHOUT THE AUTUMN OF 1966, I read many more reports than I wrote. Mainland Chinese turmoil was hot copy. Hong Kong news was not. Mr. Olson instructed me to follow the doings of the Executive and Legislative Councils, neither of which boasted a single elected member. Their purpose was to advise the governor of a colonial administration that was notably distant from the governed.

The Executive Council was dominated by very senior ex-officio government officers, with a handful of appointed representatives from the tycoon community. The Legislative Council was divided between other officials and socially prominent "unofficials" also appointed by the governor, purportedly to convey popular desires.

Two of the most interesting people in public life were notable gadflies, Elsie Elliott and Brook Bernacchi. They were the most vocal of the ten elected members of the Urban Council, a twenty-six-member body dominated by its ex-officio and appointed members. In 1965, Elliott, Bernacchi, and the other elected members were chosen by a tiny segment of the population, 6,492 actual voters. More than 200,000 of the colony's citizens were considered to have been eligible to vote, but the vast majority did not bother to register. The Urban Council was the only body which contained any elected members at all, and its responsibilities were limited to oversight of garbage collection and the City Hall where I had performed, along with some other municipal services.

Bernacchi was a lawyer and the founder of the Reform Club, a mostly expatriate group that advocated more elected representatives in government and better social services. Elliott was an English-born social activist who made no effort to conceal her disdain for colonialism. She had aroused the unending ire of the government by collecting 20,000 signatures petitioning the government to reject the Star Ferry Company's application for a fare increase for the first-class upper-deck passengers on those ferries that provided the splendid and essential harbor crossing. Some blamed her for instigating two days of rioting after the government approved the increase in April 1966. When Don Ferguson briefed me months later he said, "Those riots were a tempest in a teapot." He did not accord the incident anything like the historical importance attributed to them by academic researchers decades later. I was too new to know better.

Elsie Elliott and others berated the government's callous disregard of horrible labor and social welfare conditions and called for the enactment of decent legislation. She was howling in the dark, as she continued to do for much of her 102-year life. The advisory councils were dominated by business leaders who had no difficulty persuading the influential financial secretary, John J. Cowperthwaite, that more stringent labor laws would destroy Hong Kong's competitiveness and be a crippling burden on the budget.

I believed the leaders were honest about the challenges of enforcing a regime fair to labor in an environment where unregistered small factories were legion, but their arguments were also self-serving. Hong Kong manufacturing was a free-for-all where abundant labor for low skilled jobs kept wages low. Elliott and others were morally outraged. Those voices in the colonial heart of darkness let there be no doubt that Hong Kong in the 1960s was the ultimate cheap-labor exploitation economy. On the way to that winter of 1966–67 they gave me fodder for tidbits in the Weeka.

Such were the political doings of the time. There was not much that would become memorable besides Mao's Little Red Book, which many considered far more laughable than threatening. We did not see US interests in Hong Kong as being directly threatened by events across the border in China. We valued Hong Kong for its trade and as a port of call for our warships taking a break from the Vietnam conflict, but the highest value of the colony to the US was as a base for spying on China.

Since we had no diplomatic or other contacts of consequence with the Mao regime, we had to rely on Chinese media reports, travelers' tales and the efforts of the intelligence community. Hong Kong was the place to be for all that. For me, what my colleagues in the Political Section learned about the social implosion and Red Guard explosions of the rapidly unfolding Cultural Revolution was all but unimaginable, incomprehensible and insane.

CHAPTER 19

Macau Capitulates

L IKE DON FERGUSON, I paid no attention to Macau beyond its attractiveness as a pleasant change of scene for a weekend. Casinos were prohibited in Hong Kong, so the Portuguese colony was the haven for high and low rollers, as well as a very nice place to stroll and dine for a day or two. I qualified as being among the lowest rollers, but quickly lost fifty dollars. Barbara's disapproval forced me to quit though I wanted to win the money back. When we got back to Hong Kong I licked my wounds in the office and also reconfirmed that there was nothing in my file cabinet to show that politics in the decadent enclave was of any interest to the State Department. Money laundering and human trafficking were not terms in common use then.

A few days after Nixon left, Thomas Hui brought me an article in the Chinese press about demonstrations at the Macau governor's residence following a fracas at a construction site on Taipa, one of the colony's outlying islands. If there was anything about the incident in the local English-language press, I had missed it.

I took this as an opportunity for language practice and asked Thomas Hui to summarize the article for me in Cantonese. He read, "Leftist organizers intending to establish a private school started building without permits after their application for a license had been repeatedly rejected by the colonial government. The organizers alleged that the permits were denied because they refused to offer bribes. Police arrested the school officials and beat up construction workers, residents, and reporters on the scene."

As the demonstrations grew in size and duration, troops were called in to help the police suppress them. They didn't do very well. With the appearance of Mao-think slogans I felt that the disturbances could become a serious threat to the viability of the Portuguese colonial government. This would merit more than a few sentences written up for the Weeka.

I scrambled to learn what I could about Macau, which until then had been just a gambling haven and isle of wonder connected to the Chinese Mainland by a narrow causeway and hundreds of years of intimate relations. The population was mostly Chinese, while the Portuguese rulers and Macanese creoles lived lives that were clearly separate, yet intimately entwined with the Chinese majority. Each had their space. The waterfront along the quay from the ferry pier southward to the tip of the peninsula was distinctively Mediterranean, with a wide esplanade bordering the water and stately structures for the Portuguese elite across the roadway. The Macanese creoles had their own district to the northeast. In stark contrast, the inland center of the peninsula was jam-packed with Chinese structures that seemed to be trying to climb on top of each other.

Macau was the first European outpost on the China coast. For centuries it had been the major entrepôt for trade between Europe and southern China. Portuguese traders had been plying the area since the early sixteenth century. The first Portuguese outpost has been dated as far back as 1506, and Lisbon obtained a leasehold for Macau in return for tribute paid to Peking in 1557.

The sixteenth-century Portuguese settlers were traders who had undertaken the long and dangerous voyage around the Horn of Africa. Taking along a wife was unthinkable in those days, so the men found women among the Chinese. Some local women may have seen opportunity and status in the traders. Others apparently traded their bodies for goods, a tradition that persisted for centuries. The result of these liaisons was a mixed-blood community that was generally looked down upon by the Portuguese elite, but it was the mulattos who manned the police force and the military detachment. As the protectors of those at the top of the social and racial colonial order, they often had sinecures with plenty of opportunity for corruption. That was the glue that held the mixed-blood Macanese and their Portuguese rulers together.

Macau prospered with Portuguese power, and declined with it also. After China ceded Hong Kong to the British in 1841 as a consequence of the First Opium War, the new colony rapidly became the principal entrepôt for East-West trade, while Macau eventually became a gambling haven and vice den for visitors from Hong Kong.

Until told I was responsible for reporting on it, I knew nothing about Macau. It was a backwater of such small consequence to US interests that we had no presence there.

We theoretically handled affairs with the Portuguese colony from Hong Kong, but there was little official contact. The consul general and I were the only people accredited to the Macau government, but there was no intent to have me deal with Portuguese officials, and the consul general had no time for that. The only purpose of my visit as vice consul was to ascertain that Chinese-American retirees who had returned to the homeland were receiving their social security checks.

The disturbances came to a head on December 3, 1966, when the government ordered that demonstrators be arrested. That brought on more protesters, who sacked the colony's legislature, the Leal Senado. By the end of the day the crowds had driven the police from the streets, and there was little doubt that the targets of mob ire were the symbols of Portuguese colonial authority.

Martial law was declared. Portuguese troops were called in to enforce a curfew, but the rioting persisted for days. Eight protesters were shot dead. Several hundred were injured as police and military units broke up the ongoing demonstrations. Communist-controlled newspapers featured the carnage and issued a set of demands which would require the Portuguese to give up all but the titular trappings of sovereignty in Macau.

Local communist leaders called on the Chinese community to adopt a "three no's" approach and continue their struggle with the government—no taxes, no service, no selling to the Portuguese. After a few days it was clear that the communists had control of the situation and they meant business. Paralyzing demonstrations would continue until the government surrendered and accepted the terms imposed.

Governor Nobre de Carvalho quickly accepted communist demands that senior police and military officers responsible for the carnage be sacked. He sought to negotiate other demands, but gained little as the communists ratcheted up the pressure. Ultimately, the colonial government gave in. Agreements concluded with local leftist and PRC representatives on January 29, inflicted maximum humiliation on the Portuguese government. The terms included an official apology from the governor and acknowledgement in effect that continued colonial rule was at the pleasure of China. The Portuguese authorities renounced the use of force and agreed to compensate the families of the dead and injured. They also acceded to the demand that Chinese Nationalist (KMT) activities be banned.

The colonial government had abjectly surrendered and communist representatives with ties to Canton and Peking would now be the real authorities in Macau.

With a great deal of information translated for me by Thomas Hui, I could report that the communists did what was necessary to restore order in a population that was genuinely agitated by the killings. A key factor propelling rage against the government was the widely held belief that the police had deliberately aimed at the demonstrators to kill. It certainly looked that way to me when Thomas Hui showed me the X-ray photos of victims' skulls that were splashed all over the leftist newspapers in Hong Kong.

CHAPTER 20

Why China Didn't Take Macau Back

SHORTLY AFTER ORDER had been restored, I went to Macau to see what I could learn. Instead of the leisurely stroll down the Mediterranean-like Praia Grande, I headed toward the central city. Some shops along the way were shuttered, but once in the center of town the streets were full of people and business seemed brisk.

At the principal crossroads a large banner strung across two light poles announced an exhibition devoted to the Portuguese police atrocities. I went into the hall to find myself in a crowd of people three and four deep, gaping at pictures of the dead displayed on the walls. Life-size X-ray photos showed holes in the skulls of victims where the bullets had struck. They were identical to what I had seen in the papers during the height of the crisis.

I was mesmerized by these skulls shot at close range, execution style. It took a while before I noticed people staring at me. A quick glance. I was the only Caucasian in the hall. Murmurs, then an eerie silence. The chanting began. *"Hyut jai, hyut jai."*

Could this be Cantonese for "a little blood," the *"jai"* being the diminutive? I stiffened, tight as rigor mortis. Blood was blood, but I didn't know the Chinese to use irony.

A man dressed in a black suit and tie approached. The crowd let him pass. He came up and took my arm, then guided me quickly through the exhibit as the chanters made way and stood sullenly by. Then he led me into an office and identified himself as the director of the benevolent association sponsoring the exhibit. "Very sorry, but you should not stay. The dead too recently buried, the pain still too fresh. The inquest is still going on. People are very angry. They could become irrational." He hustled me out through a rear door, back into the tranquil street.

Safely back in Hong Kong, I asked Lung Sing about *hyut jai*. "I knew they were angry but why would they call all those pictures of bullet holes in skulls a little blood?"

Lung's brow looked like it would cover his eyes completely. "What are you talking about? The *jai* that signifies the diminutive of the preceding noun is a rising tone, but a lower flat tone produces the word meaning debt. The crowd was chanting 'Blood debt.'"

"Oh." Wrong again about those complicated Cantonese tones.

There was much to report. Though the facts were clear, speculation was in order, as is often the case in diplomatic reporting. The deputy chief of mission, Allen Whiting, called me up to the front office to discuss my draft report after Mr. Olson had cleared it. "I have information from other channels that Lisbon offered to turn Macau over to Chinese sovereignty."

Portugal evidently realized that its only future in Macau would be as executor of Chinese communist intentions for the territory. China refused the offer, leaving the Portuguese nominally in charge and profoundly humiliated. The whole affair was treated in the Macau press the way China wanted it to be treated, as a great victory of the masses over their foreign oppressors.

It seemed odd that communist China would reject the opportunity to welcome Macau and its largely Chinese population back to the embrace of the motherland. The PRC had devoted much energy in the international arena to propagandizing against the West and promoting the overthrow of colonial regimes. I thought the only way to decipher this bizarre behavior was to consider it in the Hong Kong context. Allen Whiting had advised me to think out of the box.

There was no indication that the population of Macau would resist a Chinese takeover, or that China would have difficulty governing Macau through its nominees already in place. Chinese community leaders in the colony had long standing ties with counterparts in nearby Canton, and they already dominated gambling, the mainstay of the economy.

Macau was not particularly important to China, even less so with effective control already in the hands of its local nominees. Taking Macau offered little reward while risking destabilizing Hong Kong. The British colony was China's most important trading link with the West and its principal conduit for embargoed items. That was not something to sacrifice lightly on the altar of ideological purity.

We surmised that taking Macau after a staged uprising would convey a message that Hong Kong would be next in line for restoration to the communist motherland. Macau, Hong Kong, and Taiwan were all claimed by China. Peking repeatedly stated its intent to recover them. The unanswered question was "When?" Hong Kong and part of Kowloon were ceded to the British in perpetuity, while the lease on the New Territories would not expire until 1997. As the Cultural Revolution raged, would the Mao leadership or those faction leaders who would overturn it want to destabilize Hong Kong and take it back in the near future?

It seemed logical that Peking declined Portugal's offer in order to send a clear message that China had no immediate designs on Hong Kong. The colony was much more valuable in British hands than in their own.

CHAPTER 21

Apprentice No Longer

NOT LONG AFTER I SUBMITTED my reports on the Macau crisis, the FSO originally assigned as the Hong Kong/ Macau political officer finally showed up. Alfred Harding was short and squat, mostly bald, often smiling for no particular reason. He was someone you might imagine as a jovial small-town postmaster who knows everyone by their first name. We chatted in Cantonese when we were introduced, as if we wanted to let it be known that we shared a secret language no other American in the consulate general could understand. "I haven't had the opportunity to use it in more than ten years," he said. "Who knows how much I would remember?"

Turning to English, Al gave me an account of his home leave on horseback in Scandinavia with his Danish wife. He had had enough unused leave on the books for a long vacation and beamed with pride that he finally got to use it. "We earn that leave and ought to be able to take it. The Foreign Service is full of people who feel compelled to give it up. Don't forfeit leave because some boss is desperate for your body."

Al was entitled to take his home leave, but it cost him his assignment. As best as I could tell, he was totally

unperturbed at the news that he was not to be the Hong
Kong/Macau political officer after all.

Several months before I met Al Harding, the deputy
chief of mission had called me up to his office. Allen
Whiting was obviously very busy, but his wrinkled expression of seriousness morphed into a smile. "We're going
interrupt your orientation schedule of rotating assignments
and leave you in place, at least until Harding arrives. . . ."
He frowned. "That is, if he arrives at all. We still haven't
heard a word from him."

That was a very brief meeting. By the time Harding
finally arrived, I had been called up to the office several
times to discuss reporting on the Macau crisis, giving me
an opportunity to know Whiting better.

He became a star in the China-watching firmament with
the publication of *China Crosses the Yalu* in 1960. The book
was considered to be the definitive study of China's entry
into the Korean War. It led to an appointment as the East
Asian Office director in the State Department's Intelligence
and Research Bureau while he was still in his thirties. He
was at the top of the China-watching heap when he was
assigned to Hong Kong.

Whiting was short and wiry, but the way he cocked his
head gave the impression he was taller than he actually was.
He had a well-earned reputation as an intense hard charger,
and was also known for cutting off people whose intellect
he didn't respect. I had a hunch that explained Lynn Olson's
sour disposition. Why he was so friendly to me from the
outset was a bit of a puzzle, because the norm was that
deputy chiefs of large missions are far too busy to have time
for new trainees.

I suspected that might be the professor in him. He wanted somebody pliable to mentor. When he learned that Harding would be arriving in a few days, he called me in. "Nice work on Macau. Your reporting has earned you the job. Congratulations." No more rotational training assignments.

He assigned Harding to the Political Section, which was, in effect, the China-watching section. This was highly unusual, as an inspection team would remark later. Such permanent assignments were made by the Bureau of Personnel in Washington, not by the missions overseas. The Hong Kong/Macau political officer position I was now to occupy for the rest of my so-called training assignment was three grades and years of sweat above my personal rank of FSO-7. It was the equivalent of putting an Army first lieutenant into a job for a lieutenant colonel. Even though I would be promoted quite rapidly, it still was another six years before I attained the FSO-4 rank accorded to my job now, at my first post.

This was most unlike the hemming and hawing "Fudge Factory" behavior I had seen during my brief stint in the State Department before coming out to Hong Kong. Whiting took authority into his own hands and did the sensible thing. Al Harding was an experienced Chinese language officer in Mandarin as well as Cantonese. He could read Chinese and I could not. The affable man I had displaced could offer value to the Political Section, while I would be useless to a group of analysts who spent their days poring over Chinese publications. Whiting's decision to switch our assignments gave us both useful work. It saved me from being a trainee passed along from section to section in a large mission to run errands and watch from the sidelines.

CHAPTER 22

CIA Insight

THE CHINA WATCHERS were stretched to the limit trying to keep up with the leadership struggles in Peking and Red Guard chaos throughout the country. Richard Nethercutt, Burton Levin and their colleagues worked late to slake the State Department's insatiable thirst for every tidbit they could discover. Their less sensitive reports were shared in a "cable file" with the economic and other sections, in hopes that everybody would have a general idea of what was going on.

I needed to know enough about developments in China to mine the larger meaning of what happened in Macau and ascertain whether Hong Kong would be left alone. I was left in my cubicle to read the cable file, but was last on the distribution list. The more senior officers in the section often sat on that file forever. Burt Levin came to the rescue, letting me know about major developments. He would call, "Got a few minutes, come on over and we'll share some scuttlebutt." Burt was indispensable to my education.

Unbeknown to any of us an extraordinary accolade for a report written by a gentleman that I would not meet until four months later appeared in a memo to President Johnson dated Washington, January 25, 1967. Just as I was reporting on the Portuguese capitulation to the communists in Macau!

Special Assistant Walt Rostow wrote to the president: "This is the best single reconstruction I have read of the inner politics of mainland China in this crisis. It is written by Bill Wells, an imaginative, scholarly, bold CIA man in Hong Kong."

At the risk of not giving Bill Wells due credit, I'll condense his report here to give a much abbreviated picture of the turmoil that was engulfing China.

SUBJECT: China—The Three Kingdoms Revisited

. . . There is no longer doubt of the power struggle between Mao and Lin Piao on one hand and Liu Shao Ch'i and Teng Hsiao-P'ing on the other; we have learned of the Central Committee Meeting in October (which lasted seventeen days) and to which Mao and Lin made two remarkable speeches. We have heard Lin compare Mao's struggle to keep control of the Central Committee to Stalin's struggle for power, and admit that the bourgeois advocates in the Central Committee remain in the dominant position in a number of fields. Mao in turn admits to great loss of control in the party, but makes it clear that he intends to grasp full power again whatever the cost. . . .

Whether Mao will succeed in fully restoring his control will depend a great deal on whether or not he and Lin Piao can reestablish their control of the party apparatus. . . .

China at mid-January appeared to be two circles of
political power. One circle is dominated by loyal subor-
dinates of Lin Piao and the army, although there is
great confusion at every level. In the other circle the
party apparat reigns but barely rules. . . . Each official is
now thinking of alliance and of regional defense until
the legitimate rule of the Communist Party is rees-
tablished under Mao or any other leader who will
reaffirm his predominance in his region. They have not
reached the point in political time where separate states
are thought possible. This spring, however, may bring a
consideration of this possibility.

Historic parallels are never exact although this time
events insist on historic comparison. Some things have
changed forever. The grim fact of China's huge contemporary population guarantees little time for the fun of
political misadventure. Food prices are rising in
Canton. We have no way of estimating how badly the
transport of food within China has suffered under the
vast movement of Red Guards, the forced transport
stoppages of the recalcitrant work teams or their battles
with the municipal Red Guards, and now through the
onslaught of rebel revolutionaries. The tie-ups, however, must have been and must be massive. . . . Without
transport China would not merely suffer the ravages of
1961's malnutrition, but the hell of starvation.
Moreover, China at mid-month is bitterly cold. Hong
Kong shivers in the worst cold of a decade. Human
dislocation, rising prices, short rations and cold are
Mao's new enemies.

It is, moreover, difficult to assess how long Mao and
Lin can . . . travel the same road. Lin must know that
so many of the vital managers of the party have been
arrested, insulted and ridiculed, that his power position
is in jeopardy. . . .

Mao's recent accusations flick like a snake's tongue; no
one is immune—the reorganized propaganda department, the newspapers, his fellows on the cultural
revolution subcommittee, even his most old and
trusted ministers. Lin will have an increasingly difficult
time organizing the cultural revolution while his
mentor purges follower after follower.

In Chinese history the era of the three kingdoms is an
interregnum, a period of warring anarchy despised by
the classical Chinese historian, who prefers the established dynasty with its cultural grace. In our last
analysis we suggested that China's anarchical period
would not last long for historic reasons. We still believe
this. Nevertheless it is worthwhile to look back 1600
years to the time when China divided into the three
great states of Shu, Wu and Wei, and when the art of
political intrigue reached its height. As short-lived as
the modern divisions may be, they will be with us in
1967 when a series of Chinese bravos will pass across
the face of the nation until one, shrewder than the rest,
assumes command.

I never saw this CIA document until I did research for this book, and don't know whether the State Department's Political Section people saw it either. CIA missions overseas had their own separate communications channels, and the spy agency had a long history of keeping their information and operations very close to the chest. It was entirely up to the station chiefs whether they would share information with the diplomats, and later congressional investigations showed that normally they did not.

It wasn't long before I would learn that Bill Wells was not your normal CIA officer.

CHAPTER 23

Hong Kong Simmers

B Y THE TIME WELLS' REPORT reached President Johnson and Macau's governor signed the *mea culpa* capitulation agreements, attention in Hong Kong was turning to the Chinese New Year. Factories threw year-end parties and announced bonuses for their workers with music blaring so loud that it was almost impossible to converse at the celebratory meal. When the Year of the Sheep arrived on February 9, 1967, most businesses shut down for five days of festivities with family in order of Confucian precedence: parents and grandparents first, then siblings, then friends. In many rural areas celebrations would continue until the Lantern Festival, two weeks after the first day of the new lunar year.

Once the holidays were over, it became clearer that life in Hong Kong was changing. The Cultural Revolution was being thrust into public consciousness by frequent headlines in the local press, particularly in the nine newspapers controlled by communist organizations and Peking sympathizers. Clerks in the Chinese emporia, reporters for the *Ta Kung Pao,* Bank of China employees, leftist union members, and others carried their copies of Mao's Little

Red Book to read on the Star Ferry while they crossed the harbor on the way to work. What had been laughed at was becoming a symbol of a brotherhood of discontent with an uncaring colonial government. When I encountered a group of clerks chanting Mao slogans outside a China Products Emporium I stopped scoffing.

The PRC-appointed leaders of communist organizations in Hong Kong enjoyed freedoms they could not have dreamed of when they were working in the homeland hierarchy. They could behave like free-market true believers, pursuing profit and hard currency as avidly as the most successful capitalists. Communist China had built up a network of more than 300 businesses and banks in the colony. They operated trading companies pushing Chinese goods into world markets, travel agencies to attract people to China, and markets essential to Hong Kong's food supply, as well as markets for carved ivory, jade, jewelry and antiques both real and fake. The communist businessmen proved to be very good "bourgeois capitalist roaders."

My colleagues in the economic section estimated that Hong Kong's communist enterprises were providing Peking with more than $500 million in hard currency annually. The Hong Kong dollar's peg to the pound sterling (and after 1972, to the US dollar) and unfettered currency markets facilitated the transfer of funds vital to China's foreign trade. Along with remittances from overseas Chinese, Hong Kong's Bank of China was believed to provide more than half of China's foreign currency reserves.

The head of the New China News Agency was considered to be the senior Peking official in Hong Kong, but my Foreign and Colonial Office friend Emrys Davies speculated that the real power center was the Bank of China. Regardless who was the headman among local communist leaders, they all enjoyed the stability of the colony even as the people who appointed them were being denounced as revisionists and traitors in Peking.

Burt Levin brought me into his office one spring morning to share ideas. "What do you think? Might the purges in Peking and communist success in forcing Macau to kowtow be giving Hong Kong's communist leaders plenty to worry about? Those guys are appointees from China and they haven't lifted a finger to show their zeal for Mao except to distribute that Little Red Book."

"So, would doing nothing in Hong Kong risk provoking accusations of bourgeois revisionism?" I asked.

"That's what I'm thinking," said Burt. "That could result in recall, denunciation, and the end of their careers, maybe their lives."

Sitting there in Burt's office just after Hong Kong ushered in the Year of the Sheep, I believed that Peking had made it clear in its convoluted way that refusing to take back Macau when offered was a clear signal that Hong Kong wouldn't be touched. But the internal workings of the communist cadre in Hong Kong were behind an opaque veil.

Burt had introduced the possibility that fear of not showing enthusiasm for the Cultural Revolution motivated Hong Kong's communist leaders to raise the propaganda noise level and make Hong Kong look like the land of the Red Book. That would be no easy task in the principal refuge from China's upheavals. Communist organizers faced daunting obstacles whenever they sought political support in the wider community.

In the early months of 1967, labor disputes gave the communists an opportunity. Pressures had been rising for better wages and working conditions, but government provided no real protection for laborers. They could be sacked with one day's pay when they tried to negotiate better conditions.

The small-scale labor disputes characteristic of the times did not attract my attention, and it looked like the communist leaders didn't pay much attention to them either. It was enough to report that the HKG ignored the calls for reform from Elsie Elliott and Brook Bernacchi. The government was reluctant to enforce or strengthen labor laws and left it to those involved in these disputes to settle them, much to management's advantage.

In the early spring of 1967 I was aware that tensions in labor relations had simmered just below the surface for quite some time, but frequent labor-management conflict seemed to be the norm in the colony's sweatshop economy. I was among the many who were slow to sense that labor disputes might be pointing to big trouble ahead. You might think that the flood of Mao's Little Red Book would have been a trigger to alert us, but it had seemed to be just another sign that Mao was truly crazy.

CHAPTER 24

Newsweek Reporters

I GOT A CALL FROM *Newsweek's* Sydney Liu, asking for an appointment to meet a newly arrived correspondent named Maynard Parker. I wasn't happy about somebody stealing my name, but warmed up to his proposal for lunch together at a high-class restaurant in Causeway Bay. "We would like to get acquainted and have your thoughts about the current situation."

"You mean a *tour d'horizon?*"

"Exactly. A leisurely one. Lunch is our way of saying thank you for your time."

I was not one to turn down a good meal. *Newsweek* must have a budget for that.

Maynard and Sydney were waiting for me at a restaurant entrance announcing elegance; the two reporters framed by a set of elaborately carved wood panels depicting scholars drinking wine in a garden overlooking a gorge in the mountains.

Maynard was tall and beginning to bulk a bit. Balding, he looked to be around forty. As it turned out, he was not yet twenty-seven, two years and a day younger than I. He would be one of the most inquisitive people I have ever met, a big man with big brains and a wide range of contacts.

Sydney Liu appeared to be about fifty and a bit worn, perhaps by a hard life in China. When Maynard and I spoke, it seemed as if Sydney was deep in thought.

Along with fine European table settings that seemed to include chopsticks only as an afterthought, the restaurant offered numerous traditional delicacies you would not find at your typical House of Choy in the US. Maynard and Sydney insisted that I make the difficult choices between shark's fin and bird's nest, roast suckling pig or Peking duck. I begged the two of them to help. Finally Maynard and I ganged up on Sydney. "You're the only one here who knows how to order."

We joked about the recent holiday. "If you want peace and quiet on the Chinese New Year, go to a battlefield in Vietnam," said Maynard.

"I woke up thinking it was machine-gun fire. They hung the firecrackers from the roofs in long strings and the rat-tat-tat went on nonstop for five days running. I don't know how anybody could sleep through that."

"It's that way every year," said Liu.

We discussed Macau at that first meeting, agreeing that the local China-oriented leadership restored order quickly and appeared to be in effective control. I asked about the latest developments in China. Both of them were better informed than I.

We also talked about a growing sense of uncertainty in Hong Kong that spring of 1967. "More than usual," opined Sydney Liu, "though Hong Kong has always been sensitive to developments in China. The border that separates us is a small stream no more than a few yards wide in places. China could cross it any time."

Maynard, Sydney Liu, and I would lunch together frequently in the months to come, as comrades in information sharing and analysis, and soon as good friends.

CHAPTER 25

Labor Strife Boils Over

IN EARLY MAY 1967 two major factory disputes were underway, although only one of them garnered significant press attention at the outset. The first was about new work rules issued by the Hong Kong Artificial Flower Works on April 13. The company was one of the largest of hundreds of plastic flower factories, with more than 1,000 employees who were upset with rules changes that amounted to pay cuts. Talks went nowhere. The company shut down some operations and dismissed about half the workforce two weeks later. The severance of one day's pay was all that was required by labor regulations.

The sacked workers protested outside the factory. The company got the police to intervene when demonstrators tried to block a shipment of finished goods. Police cordoned off the area to allow the shipment. Onlookers threw stones and bottles. Scuffles ensued.

It wasn't until headlines on May 7 about the previous day's melee that it became evident that this was something more than the typical Hong Kong labor dispute. Leftist papers alleged police brutality and government collusion with the factory owners when all the workers originally wanted was negotiations on the new work rules.

Over the next several days the leftist Rubber and Plastic Workers Union and the Federation of Trade Unions joined in accusations of deliberate suppression of the workers and demanded compensation for the injured, punishment of police perpetrators, and no more government interference in labor disputes. It was only after those unions got involved that we saw references to people armed with Mao's Little Red Book chanting slogans and expressing the will to fight the imperialist oppressors. Ironically, the fired workers were members of a union controlled by the Nationalists, not by the communist unions that came out in support.

The second factory dispute initially commanded much more public attention. Workers at the Green Island Cement Company protested that two European engineers assaulted two Chinese workers. Management countered that it was the workers who assaulted the engineers. By May Day the entire workforce had gone on strike, demanding large pay increases and better working conditions. Over the ensuing days the scene turned ugly. Management shut down the factory and the workers mounted demonstrations.

When reporters and a television crew tried to cover the strike, they were first threatened, and then attacked during sizeable demonstrations which spread in the vicinity of the factory. The fracas was featured in TV news reports and headlined in the newspapers. The factory union wouldn't negotiate and management would not give in under the threat of violence.

Demonstrators popped up with Mao's Little Red Book at both the cement factory and the artificial flowers factory, as well as at the sites of communist unions. Media coverage focused public attention on the disputes and demonstrations as the growing use of Maoist catchphrases suggested more trouble ahead.

Later we thought it surprising that the communist apparatus in Hong Kong took so long to capitalize on these events. It was only after the dispute at the Artificial Flower Works had festered for some three weeks that so-called comfort missions were sent to both factories. Then the confrontations took on Cultural Revolution characteristics that targeted the Hong Kong government rather than the workers' grievances.

It was as if there was a tacit agreement between the competing Communist and Nationalist unions that the little Red Book of Mao's sayings was a useful tool for expressing anger at the intransigent imperialists, but it is very doubtful that these strikers harbored dreams of bringing down the colonial regime. That kind of escalation was yet to emerge.

As Sydney Liu and I strolled into dusk and eerie quiet on Tung Tsing Street that May 11, neither of us had any idea that the tension outside the gates of the artificial flowers factory had already exploded into a serious riot. Police were chasing several thousand rioters into the resettlement estates, warrens where five people were packed into each 120-square-foot room. A mob materialized and set fires so suddenly that I did not absorb the fact that I saw nobody chanting Mao slogans. No Little Red Books. No placards

protesting the unfair treatment of the factory workers. This
was a mob, not a demonstration.

Hundreds of people poured into the street that was so
calm just a minute ago. There was no place we could duck
and hide quickly enough. I had been at work earlier in the
day, and wore a white shirt and good trousers. Clearly the
outsider. *Baak pei jyu*—white-skinned pig. I didn't belong
there. Surrounded in seconds. Sydney Liu didn't belong
there either, but when I broke and tried to run he melted
into the confusion and made his way to the airport.

The papers informed me about the extent of the riots
the next day. More than 600 police were sent to the factory
in an attempt to maintain order. Clashes broke out around
3:30 p.m. and the police fired tear gas and wooden pellets
into the crowd. Leftist newspapers alleged that the riot
police beat workers and students with batons and gun
handles, and fired gunshots. Police could not control the
spread of the rioting into the resettlement estates. A curfew
was imposed on the factory and resettlement estate areas at
9:30 p.m. but confrontations continued until past mid-
night. Some newspapers claimed that more than 10,000
rioters took to the streets, but it was impossible to ascertain
how many with any degree of accuracy. The communist-
controlled press accused the British authorities of persecution
and fascist atrocities. The death of a teenager in the area
where I was trapped was reported later.

A byline report by Charles Mohr dominated the front
page of the *New York Times* on May 12. Mohr did a careful
report based on information from a government spokesman
and allegations in the two principal communist-owned
newspapers. But he was dead wrong on one point. He

wrote, "Although the area was near the Hong Kong Airport, foreign tourists, American servicemen on rest and rehabilitation leaves, and other non-Asians were not in danger." Later I met Charles Mohr and trusted him with a story—much to my regret.

In those minutes of terror as the howling crowd ran by, nobody pointed at the foreigner cowering in the space between the buildings. An eerie quiet returned, casting a pall on my fear. When could I hope to get out of this hell?

Several eternities later I worked my way back through the womb passage that had protected me. The street was dark and deserted, like no place I'd ever seen in Hong Kong before. I tried to melt into the building façades. Stay as far away as possible from anybody real or imaginary that might appear in the distance. Get to the Hung Hom ferry that took me across the harbor when I was studying Cantonese. Go past the small shops whose bored shopkeepers let me foist my elementary Cantonese on them.

It strikes me that fright can sear memory, etching it deeply into grooves. A needle will play it like a 33-rpm record, over and over for a lifetime. But the trauma can also reduce memory to ashes. Fifty years after the events I describe here, being trapped in the mob and the words exchanged there are clear, but the details of my desperate wordless effort to get home safe are a hollow void. Emerging from where I hid, I might as well have been a small animal frozen in terror in the headlights of an oncoming car.

CHAPTER 26

More Pregnant Than Ever

WHEN I GOT HOME Barbara looked more pregnant than ever. Just two days earlier the doctor told her the baby could come any time. Her volleyball belly of last month looked like a basketball belly now. Ice in her voice. "Call Mr. Whiting."

She stared hard at the shredded remains of my shirt. "What happened to you? They've already called twice and they wouldn't tell me what's going on. They just said call as soon as I heard anything from you. Why didn't you tell me you were coming home late?"

"I ran into some trouble." Barbara went pale as a sheet.

The duty officer gave me a phone number. "Call right now. They've got the two visiting senators from the CODEL up at the consul general's residence. Mr. Whiting keeps calling to ask whether we heard anything about you. He sounded like everybody is really upset."

There was a tremor in Allen Whiting's voice. "The police have been looking for you for hours. Sydney Liu told us he slipped into the crowd when you were trapped by the mob. He went to the airport. The police went there in force to get you out and they're going nuts that they can't find you.

The senators are really upset. It couldn't be a worse time for something like this to happen."

"I'm not really hurt. They crammed in so close nobody could get in a telling blow."

"You'd better take care of your wife. We only told her you were out on assignment and we needed to talk to you. We'll talk about it tomorrow."

There wasn't much to take care of. Barbara was asleep by the time I got off the phone.

Mr. Olson confronted me when I got to the office in the morning. "That was pretty stupid. Was it your dumb idea?"

"No sir. Mr. Whiting suggested that I have a look around to get a feel for the atmospherics. Neither Sydney Liu nor I anticipated what happened. There weren't any reports of trouble in that area." It struck me that I hadn't told Mr. Olson that I was going out. Would he have dared argue with Whiting about his suggestion?

"So you didn't anticipate anything even though you've been reporting on troubles at the Green Island Cement Factory for at least a week now." Mr. Olson's wrinkled scowl seemed to crawl up his balding pate.

"But we weren't going anywhere near the cement factory."

Mr. Olson cut me off. "Go read the papers and draft a cable for State about what's going on. Get it out today. And no mention about you being an eyewitness. We don't want to look reckless and stupid." Mr. Olson turned and went into his office, leaving me standing there.

CHAPTER 27

Riot Report

VISIONS OF DEATH at the hands of a Chinese mob were not the stuff of diplomatic reporting. Foreign Service Officers are expected to be cooler heads, objective, sticklers for the facts. Analysis must be concise and to the point, authoritative, even though the newspapers we often relied on were not.

I started drafting a cable relying heavily on reporting in the *South China Morning Post,* while Thomas Hui got busy translating reports in the Chinese-language press. By midday he provided a summary focusing on the left-leaning newspapers. As could be expected, the *Ta Kung Pao,* the principal communist newspaper, was the most vociferous in its criticism of the government. It condemned the fascist colonial police attack on a peaceful crowd, described the incident as a bloodbath, and promised that the masses would take to the streets in support of the striking workers until justice was done.

Although we had information that Mao's Red Book was not in evidence during the evening's riot, I wrote a comment that the festering factory disputes were fertile ground for Red Guard fervor to take root among the disgruntled in Hong Kong. We judged the riot to be a spontaneous outbreak, but it was evident that leftists were capitalizing on the strikes. We could well see more of this in the days to come.

I took my draft cable to Mr. Olson for clearance, expecting him to send it out as section chiefs were authorized to do. Mr. Olson barely glanced at my draft. "Take it up to Whiting. He's going to tinker with it anyway."

Mr. Whiting told me again how relieved he was to learn that I was OK. He said nothing about how angry the consul general was at his dinner for the visiting senators. Nor did he reveal that the senators were teed off, but Burt Levin did. He said they asked, "Who could be so stupid as to wander into a Chinese mob?" I also learned that this supper was marked by long stretches of distressed silence.

I gave Whiting the draft report I had labored over all day, confident that it would be read in Washington. It would be close to twenty years before CNN's live reporting would preempt anything a diplomat might write. In 1967 our cables could compete with the news services for eyeballs if we really worked fast. I was hoping for praise for a job well done.

Whiting squinted and scanned the report I spent hours on in a minute or two. I looked out the window in back of him, past St. John's Cathedral and down to the harbor, streaks of water shimmering between anchored ships. Was this all the attention my effort would get in the State Department?

My mentor-to-be snapped me out of my reverie. "You ought to be able to cut at least thirty percent of the verbiage from this report." He paused and I cringed. "It's not easy to write clear and succinct prose. Since it looks like you're going to be writing a lot of reports in the days to come, we might as well start getting it right."

I shrank back into Miss Cuthbert's and Miss Benz' English classes. Never a word of praise from those two dedicated old maids who gave me the only Cs I ever received in high school. I couldn't recall them praising anything I ever wrote.

"Take this back and cut everything that's repetitive. Then go over it again and delete whatever isn't absolutely essential. Check your organization again to make sure that everything tracks." With a flip of Mr. Whiting's hand I had been given another C.

It was 8 p.m. before I finally got a revised report to him. He slashed my effort again in no more than five minutes. "It is getting better. Take a look at these revisions. If they're OK get it typed up and we'll send it out."

I forgot to tell Barbara that I would be late. She was another day more than nine months pregnant and getting sick of it. When I rang the doorbell instead of fumbling in my pockets to find the keys, she opened the door a few inches. For a moment it seemed as if she would slam it in my face.

CHAPTER 28

Wall of Worry

THE DAYS THAT FOLLOWED started earlier than usual. I left Barbara half asleep and drove down the narrow road that snaked through low-lying fog from Magazine Gap to May Road and Garden Road to the consulate general. The *South China Morning Post* was in the office when I arrived, with its front page devoted to reports and pictures of the disturbances. Thomas Hui was already busy summarizing items in the Chinese-language press, translating *Ta Kung Pao* and *Wen Wei Po* vitriol into English so we could discuss what they might reveal about leftist intentions. The other seven left-wing papers were known mostly for tip sheets on the Jockey Club horseraces and racy scandals, but Thomas scoured them and the middle-of-the-road papers too.

Demonstrations and violence continued over the next several days, with hundreds of arrests and daily claims of atrocities committed against the Chinese people featured in the leftist press. It was communist papers that first reported a thirteen-year-old boy had been beaten to death by the police during the evening of May 11, in the area where I had been pummeled to much lesser effect.

The HKG put the British garrison on alert and called on the public to support maintenance of law and order. The left-wing Federation of Trade Unions established the All-Industries Workers Anti-Persecution Struggle Committee to lead resistance to imperialist aggression. The committee demanded that the government cease its brutality, release those arrested, pay compensation for damages, and punish the perpetrators of the violence.

A report I found jarring was that bus drivers and conductors at the Kowloon Star Ferry terminal held a Mao-think chant-in, waving their little Red Books at commuters and pasting big-character posters condemning the imperialists on the backs of their buses. The Star Ferry was the principal means of getting across the harbor, and the bus terminal there was a key transport hub. A public transport strike would be as ominous as it would be disruptive. Leftist unions were dominant in both the Kowloon bus and Star Ferry companies.

Ultimately the police were able to quell the disturbances without calling in the army garrison, but order wasn't restored until May 14.

The relief did not last long. The *Ta Kung Pao* and other papers featured threats by the Anti-Persecution Struggle Committee that the fight would continue everywhere until the government acceded to their demands. We could not imagine that the government would kowtow and release those arrested, pay damages, and punish its police force.

I arrived at the office on the morning of May 16, to learn that the confrontation had taken a new and ominous turn. Thomas Hui didn't delay to write out a translation of what he had read in the *Ta Kung Pao*. He studied the article again and summed it up for me. The PRC Foreign Ministry had summoned the British chargé d'affaires in Peking and presented the strongest protest against "fascist atrocities" committed by the Hong Kong government. Besides a litany of accusations against the police, the protest also accused the HKG of colluding with the US against China by providing Hong Kong as a base for aggression against Vietnam, and stepping up other hostile measures against China by excluding the influence of the great Cultural Revolution. The statement called for immediate and unconditional acceptance of the Hong Kong Struggle Committee's demands, plus apologies to the victims and guarantees there would be no such incidents in the future.

I checked in with Burt Levin and we climbed a wall of worry together. It was already clear that what started as a labor dispute had developed into communist-guided rage against the government, vented in the streets, the leftist press, and big-character posters denouncing atrocities. Until now, the local communist apparatus was acting on its own. At least it appeared that way. With Peking's explicit support of local demands, we could only ask whether the local tail was wagging the dog in Peking, or is it to be that Peking really intends to make a serious attempt to force Hong Kong to capitulate?

"There's no telling," opined Burt. "It's impossible to say who's in charge, much less what will happen. No doubt the Brits will take this seriously. So should we."

CHAPTER 29

Master Spy

MR. WHITING CALLED ME UP to the front office. He was not alone. As usual, he wasted no time with small talk. "Listen. Relying on press accounts for our reporting to Washington might be helpful, but it's hardly sufficient. We have to have access to more information than that."

I did not recognize the man who was with him. He was tall, bespectacled, with slightly disheveled sandy hair that showed streaks of gray. "Wild Bill" Wells greeted me warmly, as if I was a friend he had not seen in some time, but I was pretty sure we had never met. The CIA station chief smiled as we spoke. He was too relaxed to be a Foreign Service Officer in the midst of a crisis. You wouldn't take him to be a master of the spy business.

"You two will get to know each other well," said Whiting. "Here's how we'll work this."

Wild Bill Wells looked me straight in the eye. His contagious smile turned serious. "You realize that you can't source any of this stuff in your reporting. You either find the same information elsewhere, or you cloak what you write in a way that it never can be traced back to what you will be reading here."

"That's right," said Whiting. "The reports you will see remain with me here in the front office. You read them here and leave them here. It's up to you how to weave what you learn from them into what you write for me every day, but if you can't plausibly get the information elsewhere or speculate based on your own work you can't report it. That's the deal."

"If you understand and comply, we'll help each other out," added Wells. "Don't hesitate to ask if you have any questions. And remember, most of this is what other people tell us. We have to figure out whether it's worth anything or not."

Bill Wells made me feel as if I was one of his team. I was stupefied.

In those days electronic signal intelligence was not inconsequential, but the state of "sigint" then was more like ham radio than the supercomputer hacking of today. Wells was a "humint" (human intelligence) guy who had already risen to be the head of the CIA's China-watching operation in Hong Kong by the time he was forty. His work had been brought to the attention of President Johnson.

When I met him in 1967 we could only watch China from the outside. Even the Warsaw talks, periodic exchanges between the US and Chinese ambassadors to Poland, were in limbo. It would be another seven years before the two antagonists would establish liaison offices in each other's capitals, and almost thirteen before we had formal diplomatic relations. Wells' role in creating what we understood of China during those early stages of the Cultural Revolution was huge.

Watching China without direct contact was no easy task, but Hong Kong offered access to people who conducted a great deal of business with the Mainland. Travelers' tales were readily accessible from numerous contacts in the business world, from paid agents, and even in bars if you had the people to listen. Wild Bill Wells' operation cultivated people assiduously and recruited agents who could provide useful information. The details of his operation were more than ordinarily secret. He warned me that protection of his sources was essential.

This is not to say that all the information gathered was essential. As Wild Bill cautioned, "Much of what we learn is what agents and contacts want to tell us. Whether it's fact, rumor, fabrication or contrivance is another question."

That came home in its baldest form five years later when one of my tasks in our Taipei Embassy was coordinating the information that the CIA unit there was willing to share with us. A report from a "reliable well-informed source" about the Nationalist government's internal workings appeared surprisingly familiar. After some minutes searching memory I pulled out the pro-government *Lien Ho Pao* newspaper from several days earlier. There it was: identical paragraphs, in exactly the same order as the highly classified CIA report.

When I first met Wild Bill Wells, I was wide-eyed at the prospect of being given access to the secrets gathered by our spooks. He gave every impression of having graciously agreed to cooperate in the effort to keep me informed. I couldn't help being surprised, because the spy agency had a well-earned reputation for keeping its clandestine operations, like assassination attempts against unfriendly foreign leaders, to itself. There had been plenty of arguments over whether the agency's overseas operations should even be under the jurisdiction of the ambassador in our missions abroad.

The CIA stations were notorious for operating independently, and ambassadors often weren't informed about what they did. While State Department people resented this kind of secrecy, the intelligence agencies had their reasons. Officials and politicians were inveterate leakers of information that might cost agents their lives, embarrass America and our allies, or reveal sensitive sources and collection methods. Allen Whiting had previously worked closely with the CIA when in the State Department. He gave every impression of having overcome this paranoia in his relationship with Bill Wells.

I spent a lot of time every day reading the CIA take, trying to memorize it all because I could not take the reports out of the front office. The challenge was to distill the information in such a way that my own reporting could not lead back to CIA sensitive data and sources. That wasn't so easy, because everything I saw was classified to the hilt.

From time to time Wild Bill would stop by and talk to me about those reports, offering opinions and advice. He was notably affable, so unlike Mr. Olson, my sidelined boss. I was astonished that Bill Wells, already head of a major operation, treated me as a colleague and equal. In truth he was a most generous mentor, and I wasn't even CIA.

CHAPTER 30

Real and Fake Blood

T HE RESTORATION OF CALM in the streets after three days
of rioting was deceptive. Attacks on the Hong Kong
government were carried forward in the communist press.
Protests lodged locally and by the vice foreign minister to
the British chargé in Peking made it pretty clear this was
just the beginning. China's reiteration of local communist
demands was a major escalation of the confrontation. We
had not anticipated PRC involvement even a week earlier,
but now I had no difficulty getting Allen Whiting's agreement to report to Washington that there was likely to be a
lot of trouble ahead.

Evidently confident of Peking's support, the All-Industries
Anti-Persecution Struggle Committee became the All-Circles
Anti-Persecution Struggle Committee, claiming the leaders
of prominent leftist organizations as its members. Bill Wells
opined that we could not be sure that all the reported
committee members were even aware in advance that they
had been co-opted into the organization purported to
assume direction of the struggle. He said that some of his
sources believed that the shots were being called by the

head of the New China News Agency, perhaps together with the head of the Bank of China.

The Struggle Committee moved quickly, dispatching seventeen of its representatives to Government House on May 17, to demand that Governor Trench receive their protest and demands in person. The governor was not inclined to do so, though there was some debate among his advisors. The demands were essentially identical to earlier demands for capitulation.

His response had already been issued in a statement that the government's duty was to maintain law and order as fairly as possible for the benefit of everybody. The statement repeated denials of leftist claims that the government sided with companies in industrial disputes. In a clear dig to leftist calls for struggle, Governor Trench also claimed that peace and order was the wish of almost everyone in the community.

The Struggle Committee delegation was stopped at the gate. The members took to reading quotations from Chairman Mao and chanting slogans. This was all headline material for the leftist newspapers the next day. An English-language report mentioned that members of the committee arrived at Government House in Mercedes Benz sedans. The fancy cars reminded me of Jimmy Hoffa, the flamboyant Teamsters Union leader who finally had been put in prison two months earlier.

The governor refused to accept the Struggle Committee representatives' protest in person, but he did agree to allow demonstrators to march up to Government House to voice their protest so long as they did so in small groups and peacefully. Students from leftist schools were mobilized, along with employees of the numerous communist-controlled companies and organizations. On May 19, just three days after the formation of the All Circles Struggle Committee, several thousand demonstrators wearing Mao badges on their white shirts and brandishing the little Red Book snaked up the narrow Garden Road sidewalk, right past our building and on up the hill to Government House.

I stared at them through a window, close enough to be surprised by how well dressed they were. They were orderly. They did not look like the tough laborers who had rioted the week before. This was a parade of well-organized groups that were following orders.

As you might expect, the demonstrators chanted a litany of anti-British slogans. They plastered the gates of Government House with big-character posters, imitating Red Guard activities in China. The police made no attempt to stop them. So long as the demonstrations were peaceful, the government wanted to avoid any incidents that the leftist propaganda machine would surely exploit.

The nature of the demonstrations had changed since the spontaneous outpourings of workers' rage at unfair police interference in the flower factory dispute, arbitrary dismissals, and terrible working conditions. Mob formation was easy on May 11. Now, with neatly dressed school kids and apparent white-collar workers marching with their Mao badges and Little Red Books, the anger at government unfairness to labor was being led by prominent leftists with ties to communist organizations. The protests were becoming Mao-speak. For the moment, the demonstrations of Cultural Revolution zeal were peaceful, but the original intent of the factory workers to negotiate working conditions was all but forgotten.

I had too much to do in the office to stand at the window and count the number of demonstrators marching up Garden Road, but estimates were that 3,000 made the trip. Police reinforcements watched warily, but made no attempt to stop the procession.

I learned later from Emrys Davies, the assistant political advisor, that the HKG believed the not-so-long march to Government House by the masses would be a one-day affair. It wasn't. Further large-scale processions were prohibited. Delegations wishing to petition the governor were limited to no more than twenty people at a time. Tension grew. On March 22, more well-organized and well-dressed demonstrators violated the order and gathered near the foot of Garden Road to march up the hill.

Riot police ordered them to turn back, but they stood their ground. When the demonstrators tried to break the police cordon a melee ensued. Communist newspapers called the encounter a bloody massacre. The pro-government press reported that demonstrators were seen pouring red ink over themselves as the confrontation developed. The so-called massacre was faked. I think I got it right when I reported that both allegations seemed to have elements of truth. The police probably used more force than necessary against those who charged them, while much of the evidence pointing to a bloodbath was faked.

Regardless, the leftists now had an incident to exploit. Loudspeakers installed on the landmark Bank of China Building blared Maoist slogans and denounced Governor Trench. Crowds gathered in the Central business district and threw whatever they had at the police. They were met with a choking dose of tear gas. Buses and trams were abandoned. By dinnertime the government had imposed another curfew.

The battle was engaged, symbolized by ear-splitting government broadcasts of jazz and the Beatles contesting the incendiary broadcasts from the Bank of China. While the China-owned *Wen Wei Po* newspaper screamed bloody suppression, the colonial government resorted to emergency regulations to deal with the crisis. Besides the curfew, the HKG prohibited illegal broadcasting, promising heavy fines and prison for violators.

Along with reporting the unfolding confrontation in the streets, I was trying to give Washington a feel for the rhetoric accompanying the violence. For example: "The warrior equipped by the invincible Mao Tse-tung Thought would never succumb to your force. We fear neither heaven nor earth. We are not daunted by deaths. We resolutely oppose you and are unswerving in struggling with you. We will resolutely struggle against you until we overthrow you."

How much was bluff? How much was a credible threat? Would Hong Kong's leftists ultimately be able to force a capitulation like the Portuguese surrender of authority in Macau only months before? How much support did the local communist leadership have from Peking? Did huge anti-British protests in major Chinese cities signal PRC intentions?

I pondered these questions as I struggled to make my reports coherent and Allen Whiting went over them with me. We revised and updated well into the evening hours.

There was so much pressure to get the cables out in time to be on desks in Washington first thing in the morning that I forgot to call home to say I would be late. No doubt Barbara would have appreciated that. The less practical reasons for calling didn't occur to me. Dinner was cold in the refrigerator.

During those last weeks of her pregnancy, Barbara was often asleep when I got home. She was expecting that labor would have to be induced if birth did not occur soon.

If she was awake when I got home, exhaustion from nonstop excitement and the task of reporting it left little energy for discussion of what the HKG called the "emergency." And I didn't have a clue how the extended pregnancy, the crisis, and my work might be affecting her. I barely recall telling her not to worry about it.

CHAPTER 31

Finally. It's a Girl

MY CRAZY WORKING HOURS left Barbara little opportunity to express resentment that I had ventured
into a mob and risked leaving her alone to raise our child
in a foreign land where she did not speak the language.
Perhaps I didn't hear it, because the days after I got caught
in the first big riot went by in a self-absorbed blur.

I finally got a day off on June 1. Barbara woke in the
middle of the night with labor pains, but as an experienced
nurse she was far less anxious than I. "Go back to sleep.
We'll go to the hospital in the morning."

I drove her to the Hong Kong Sanatorium & Hospital,
an old established hospital near the Happy Valley racetrack
that was home to the Hong Kong Jockey Club and world-
class bettors on the horses. English was spoken at the
hospital, making it the choice for many in the foreign
community. The building was perched on a hill with great
views of the harbor and the Wan Chai District of Suzie
Wong fame.

The Sanatorium dates back to 1922, with its white-
washed interior walls hemming in narrow corridors, aged
linoleum floors scrubbed clean and bare. We were led to a

narrow sparse room to face contractions together. A bed
against the right wall and a chair against the left. The
spasms came with suppressed grunts every few minutes.
Barbara's talent at concealing pain made it seem as if this
was no big deal. The hours dragged on. I came to be as
bored with the contractions as I was excited about becoming a father. It looked like I wasn't going to get a report out
to the State Department today.

We spoke little, not drawing much on shared memories.
No doubt Barbara was dealing with much more pain than
I could imagine, but our limited conversation came as no
surprise. One of the traits I liked about her was that she did
not babble on and on like the girls I had met at Columbia's
graduate school. She did not try to out-intellectualize me,
and I appreciated her apparent distaste for small talk.
Fortuitous, since I was not much of a listener.

With Barbara I was not much of a talker either. Her
interest in my work and my music was perfunctory. She
didn't ask much about the disturbances beyond queries
about our safety. I assured her, "We're safe. The
demonstrators won't come up the hill any further than
Government House. The path is so steep that people like
us used to be carried home in sedan chairs by sweating
coolies."

As morning faded into noon I was asked to leave the
room more frequently by the nurse who checked up on
Barbara's condition. Time was measured by dilation in
centimeters.

It was mid-afternoon before Barbara was wheeled into
the delivery room. A nurse gave me a surgical gown and
mask and brought me in to witness the birth. So close I

could almost feel the final push and a few pounds of life popping out with surprising force. The doctor deftly caught our newborn and told us her umbilical cord was quite calcified. We had decided a girl would be named Ruth Leslie.

The nurse quickly cleaned Ruth up and handed her to me. After due cultural deference to the sire, she took my baby back and handed her to Barbara. Mama was drained by the effort, but that wan smile of joy was as big as I had ever seen it. We were parents.

I didn't have much time to contemplate the enormity of it. Soon again, I was reporting on demonstrators shouting Maoist slogans and throwing whatever they could at the police trying to contain them. My baby and my wife were asleep by the time I got home from work, and I would sleep through Ruth Leslie's whimpering for mama's milk in the middle of the night.

If life and motherhood in a strange city where she was safely away from the riots in an apartment halfway up the Peak was difficult for Barbara, I confess to being unaware of it. My impression was of the luxury of having a maid to take care of all the housework. In my narrow view Barbara was well taken care of by a nineteen-year-old Chinese girl who I found to be unusually attractive and smart.

CHAPTER 32

Bad News From Peking

I WAS BACK TO WORK just in time to see our appraisal of PRC intentions challenged. We had come to hope and believe that China did not really wish to cripple Hong Kong or take it back. The shocker came in two commentaries appearing consecutively in the authoritative *People's Daily* on June 2 and June 3. The first urged that Hong Kong compatriots seek repayment of blood debts: "The paper tiger British imperialists will be smashed by the storm of revolution and their doomsday will come."

The next day's editorial was more explicit, calling on Hong Kong and Kowloon compatriots "to organize, struggle and prepare to answer the call of the motherland to smash the reactionary regime of British imperialism. Armed with Mao Tse-tung thought, the Chinese are sworn to provide powerful backing to their Hong Kong compatriots." The paper proclaimed reliance on the working class as the main force of revolution. "Youth and student movements would be mobilized to merge with the workers and all compatriots to carry on the fight."

Hong Kong's leftist press paraded the *People's Daily* editorial as Peking's unconditional support for the struggle to bring the Hong Kong government to its knees.

On the face of it, this appeared to be a much clearer indication of Peking's support for struggle in Hong Kong than anything we had seen before. Was it to be taken seriously, or was this just the bluster of the most radical elements in Peking? Against a background of fierce factional infighting, Bill Wells mused that this could mask a quest for personal survival by showing devotion to eternal Cultural Revolution.

We could not know for sure. There was so much turmoil in China. My Political Section colleagues and the CIA were getting information about attempts by radical factions to displace and disgrace established leaders in key central government positions. We could not tell whether relative moderates like Chou En-lai were still able to mandate policy.

Getting huge amounts of information did not promise clarity. The fog of unknown real intentions reminded me that I had been in a similar cocoon-like situation during the Cuban Missile Crisis five years earlier. The destroyer I served on was ordered to search the Caribbean for Russian ships suspected of carrying missiles to the Castro regime. We sensed there was trouble, but had no idea how much as we searched the seas for four days and drank ourselves silly on the fifth, with movies at the Guantanamo Officers' Club on the hill and an occasional USO show. Later we joked that we came to the Bob Hope show and left to the Perry Como show, which was true.

I had access to a lot of information then because I was the cryptography officer who decoded messages all day and much of the night (sixty-four hours without relief at one point). I had to read all of those messages to verify that my typed decoding was not garbled. I can assure you that none of that trove of raw information gave me any idea how close we had come to blows with the Soviet Union.

Hong Kong in 1967 was eerily similar in that there were a lot of messages, but decoding them into real meaning was a challenge. With all the chaos even at the highest levels in China, it was no easy task to predict outcomes, despite all the accumulated experience of the China watchers.

Our analyses and bets were hedged in May 1967. We did know that China had rejected Portugal's offer to turn over its hobbled colony in Macau to PRC formal sovereignty. Why then would China's leaders want to take over Hong Kong, which was so much more valuable to them in British hands than it would be in their own?

We had to take the threats seriously, though we remained skeptical that China would act on them. At the very least, it seemed clear that local communist leaders believed that they had Peking's support for an all-out struggle to force the Hong Kong government to capitulate as Macau's had. We were so preoccupied with our crystal balls of the present that I didn't even think about what we might do if they succeeded.

We were far beyond a dispute about the abysmal labor conditions in Hong Kong. This had become an ongoing direct challenge to Britain's ability to govern. As metaphor, the Bank of China building was enclosed with a barbed wire barrier, ostensibly to defend against anticipated fascist atrocities.

Most of the time Mr. Whiting waited until I had my draft report ready before seeing me to critique it. I felt triumphant when he cleared my day's effort with only a few revisions, and took it on the chin when I missed anything he thought might be worth reporting. This time he called me up to the office mid-morning, just moments after I had finished reading Thomas Hui's translation of that June 3 editorial.

"What do you think of it?"

I told him the facts.

"What else?" He looked at me with eyes flashing a warning that I had missed something.

I pinched my chin between my right thumb and index finger. He seemed to be willing to give me a moment to think, but not much more than that. Sweat trickled down my back.

Finally. "Strange. I'm pretty sure I didn't see anything about the demands they made after the first big riots. Maybe Peking doesn't want to risk that the Brits would call their bluff. There's been no indication that the HKG has any intention of acceding to any of those humiliating demands. No apologies, no release of the arrested, no compensation."

Those glittering eyes again. "So what does it mean to you?"

"Those references to a long struggle suggest that China doesn't want to take over, but they might think it would be very nice if the local communists could humiliate the British on their own."

The penetrating gaze softened as Allen Whiting smiled. "Your analysis that this confrontation goes far beyond the labor dispute that sparked it is correct, but that's past history. What Washington will be begging for is our thoughts about where all this is going." We parried back and forth. How real is Peking's support for the locals? "See Emrys Davies for the British view and check with your other contacts. Find out what they think. That should make for a report that will get some attention in D.C."

Emrys agreed to see me the next morning. "Yes, the *People's Daily* expressed what might seem to be undying support for the Hong Kong leftists, but the editorial did not go beyond exhorting them to prepare to answer the call of the motherland at the right time," he said. "That does not seem to be now. Regardless of China's intentions, Governor Trench believes it is imperative to act forcefully to reduce the leftists' ability to create havoc. Our only choice is to suppress disturbances. Otherwise we will become another Macau. We will not kowtow to that humiliation.

"We're more confident that we can handle the disturbances than we were a couple of weeks ago. The police have shown themselves to be disciplined and loyal, even though we ordered them to stand guard behind their shields and not break up demonstrations unless they are attacked and in danger. We didn't want to give the communists another bloody incident, so we insisted on restraint."

Emrys rubbed the right side of his nose with his index finger. "It looks like the police are immune being cursed as yellow-skinned dogs doing the bidding of white-skinned pigs."

He asked if I knew about the June 1 emergency regulations that outlawed preparation, distribution and display of inflammatory materials. I nodded. Incendiary Red Guard–style posters had been plastered in many parts of the city in the days following the faked "brutal massacre" on Garden Road.

"We will not tolerate the communist version of free speech any longer. Now that forbearance has gained us expressions of public support from many civic groups, we will go on the offensive. The governor is confident that forceful action will bolster confidence that the emergency is under control."

I had thought of Emrys as a calm voice in the storm. He was getting heated now. "The police will be tasked with removing offending posters and pictures. They'll start by cleaning up the buses, trams, and ferries. We will get their propaganda off the streets."

CHAPTER 33

Sitting on the Fence

MAYNARD PARKER SAID he was as anxious as I was to get together for another *tour d'horizon* when we had lunch together that day. Like our previous meetings, the meal was a sumptuous mix of expensive specialties. I'm pretty sure we had shark's fin and bird's nest soup, a delicacy we slurped without concern for what havoc our species was wreaking on the planet.

Then there was roast suckling pig and a delicious garbage-fed chicken dish. At least these animals were not raised in the mass production cruelty that we see now. In contemporary parlance our gluttony conveyed membership in the top one percent. Rachel Carson's *Silent Spring* had yet to slap us in the face for our profligate consumption. Meanwhile Hong Kong workers in the sweatshops were being paid a dollar a day.

That wasn't our concern during these luncheons. We were into prognostications, strategies, and political gossip. Sydney Liu was with us. He jumped into the brainstorm. "Most Chinese in Hong Kong harbor strong resentment of the colonial regime, even those who left everything behind to seek safety here. The public waits to see. They are sitting on the fence, non-committal in their loyalty to the government despite its claims of overwhelming public support for emergency measures to quell the disturbances. Chinese will not be on the losing side if the British can't maintain order."

Maynard interjected. "This is as much a public relations battle as it is a fight on the streets. The communists have pasted their posters everywhere with photos of that fake blood on Garden Road. They have their newspapers and their unions and workers to participate in strikes and demonstrations." He paused to chew on a thin slice of pig's ear. "If the Brits want to stay in Hong Kong they have little choice but to get public support. They lose if they crack a lot of Chinese heads to maintain order. But there is no doubt that they will have to crack down if they're going to stay in charge."

With that, I had a great deal to think about as I nervously mulled over what I should say at next Tuesday's senior staff meeting. I was far and away the most junior participant. My situation felt akin to being a seventh-grade class president called upon to report to the Parent Teachers' Association on playground conditions.

CHAPTER 34

Reporters, Academics, Nemesis

W HEN PEKING GOT INVOLVED in the Hong Kong disturbances, reporters came to the consulate general
looking for the story. Allen Whiting arranged that reporters
would be referred to me, and gave explicit instructions:
"Make every reporter commit that conversations with you
are off the record. No attribution to you or even to 'an
unnamed American official.' You'll be asked about our view
of Chinese and British intentions. It's OK to speculate, but
only if you trust who you are talking to. If in doubt, watch
your mouth."

All that was fine by me. Being a "knowledgeable source"
cited in the news was reward enough.

The trickle of reporters and scholars became a steady
stream. I enjoyed these exchanges with people who often
had greater insight than I had information. Among those
who stood out were Stanley Karnow and Don Oberdorfer
of the *Washington Post*, Bernard Kalb, Tillman Durdin, and
Charles Mohr of the *New York Times*, and Donald Kirk of
the *Washington Star*.

Karnow was a consummate gentleman and Pulitzer
Prize–winner who covered Asia for *Time, Life*, the London

Observer, NBC News and others as well as the *Post.* He certainly had more valuable sources than I could ever have developed from my office in the consulate general. He was so modest that you would never know that. He engaged me as if my knowledge and insight were at least as valuable as his. I was more than flattered, for he was thirteen years older and his experience was measurable in multiples of that age difference. Later he wrote *Mao and China: Inside China's Cultural Revolution* (New York, NY: Penguin Books, 1984), which was nominated for the National Book Award.

Bernie Kalb and Don Oberdorfer stood out in contrast to Karnow. They were rat-a-tat sharp with their questions. It felt like an inquisition. They seemed to have preconceived ideas of what they were going to report, and asked questions designed to bring answers supporting those ideas. Much to my benefit, they had no qualms about sharing their understanding of what was happening in China, quite confident that they had a bead on the Cultural Revolution. To me, China was all convulsion and confusion.

Tillman Durdin of the *New York Times* was among the most introspective and thoughtful of journalists. An old China hand, he had been reporting from Asia since the mid-1930s, and was happy to share stories of his experience and impressions of the leaders he had interviewed over the years. I admitted to him how heavily dependent I was on Burt Levin and Thomas Hui for my meager knowledge of China. Nothing was said about the treasure trove of information that Wild Bill Wells was sharing with me in the front office.

Charles Mohr was different. He was diffident and in-gratiating, with no claims of deep knowledge or experience in Asia other than Vietnam. He was superb at gaining trust and information. The confrontation had already been going on for some two months before he called on me. I'll catch up with events before he arrived on the scene and write more about him anon.

Along with the reporters, China watchers from the academic world also were frequent visitors. Well-known professors like Robert Scalapino and Dixie Walker had spent their illustrious careers following every bit of news they could get about communist China, but they were unable to go there. They were looking to write academic think pieces and books, but had to satisfy their quest for knowledge by visiting local scholars and people like me.

With the *People's Daily* June 3 editorial, the professors and the China watchers expressed puzzlement at what appeared to be a deliberate move to destabilize Hong Kong. Why would the PRC want to destroy its single most important provider of hard currency?

I wondered whether this might just be another example of virulent propaganda, or were there really factions embroiled in the PRC leadership struggles who were pressing for a takeover? I didn't have anything close to an answer. We were far from ascertaining the motivations of the leadership in Peking, or even whether those leaders would remain in power.

The academics were always curious about my background in China studies. "Which Asian Studies Institute did you attend? Columbia's Russian Institute. What? I never took a single course on China. What brought you here? That's a long story. I'm a Hong Kong-watcher now."

Professors Scalapino and Walker joked about the irony of the accidental China watcher.

We would mull over Peking and local communist intentions. I learned a lot more from them about Mao and the madness of his revolutionary campaigns than they could hope to learn from my day-to-day immersion in Hong Kong developments.

All I could tell them was that I thought the disturbances were serious and likely to be sustained. The police were showing restraint and the general public seemed to be passive. There was no love for the Hong Kong government and its laissez-faire policies that did almost nothing for the huge struggling working class. But how could there be any public support for the leftists, since so many had come to Hong Kong to escape the yoke of Mao-think?

I don't recall acknowledging it at the time, but in retrospect the professors gave me more credit than I deserved. I was taking what information I had and playing it by ear.

I had been quite surprised when Allen Whiting told me he was going to send reporters and academics my way. As my mentor, he set my role in the mission and taught me how to play it. As the de facto chief operating officer he had already offended Mr. Olson by cutting him out of the normal chain of command. Now he had bypassed another much more senior officer when he set me up as the rapporteur dealing with the reporters.

Harvey Feldman, the US Information Agency (USIA) officer designated as the mission's press officer, was instructed by Whiting to send the reporters to me. I hardly knew Harvey. His face seemed to be pockmarked with resentment. His voice was harsh, often sarcastic. Others knew him as a cheerless but competent sourpuss. Rumor had it that he was about to be divorced by his quite beautiful wife, who was seen as a trophy of sweetness. Nobody seemed surprised about those rumors, which turned out to be true.

No doubt Harvey bristled at being cut out of the loop. Mr. Whiting had stripped him of an important part of his job.

As was the case with Mr. Olson, I was far junior to Feldman in rank, but Whiting left no doubt that he was going to work with only one guy on Hong Kong. There was too much going on in China to allow reporting on the local emergency to get mired in a fudge factory. It seemed to be the sensible thing to do.

Harvey Feldman and I spoke very little to each other. We were stiffly polite in an atmosphere of his thinly concealed arrogance and my not so genuine humility. He was to get his revenge six years later when he came to head the Political Section in our embassy in Taipei, near the end of my four-year tour as the Taiwanese political officer. I had worked for years with Taiwanese activists agitating for reform and democracy, while he was a newcomer establishing authority over his section. The one thing I'm sure we could agree on was that we didn't like each other from the outset. It mattered little whether I might be right in my analysis or reporting. In Taipei, he evaluated my performance, not vice versa. It was clear to me that the mutual distaste found its origins in our relationship in Hong Kong.

By that later time I felt that the great veneer of civility I saw in the Foreign Service cloaked an extremely competitive group of people chasing a paucity of promotions. In

Hong Kong I could ignore Harvey Feldman. In Taipei I could not. Although I had few friends in the Foreign Service because I found many of my colleagues to be rather boring pedants, Feldman was the only FSO I came to detest.

CHAPTER 35

Life Goes On

A S HOT HUMID DAYS of confrontation dragged on with demonstrations, strikes and rumors that communist China would take over the colony, daily life became a challenge of avoiding trouble in one of the most crowded cities in the world. June brought more demonstrations and threats in the leftist press, along with claims of injuries and deaths at the hands of police.

Despite moments of apprehension, it turned out to be rather easy to avoid trouble. Go to the office in the morning and head directly for home after the long days of gathering information and reporting it. Most of my meetings were in the office, and those outside were in parts of town we were reasonably certain would be safe.

Perhaps I was blasé in the comforts of my office and our Coombe Road apartment halfway up Victoria Peak, but the demonstrators did not march up those steep hills. Nor did they come back to Garden Road again, though blocking access to the Peak Tram terminal across the street from the consulate general would have caused major inconvenience to commuters and bad press for one of Hong Kong's favorite tourist attractions.

There was no question of sending me out again to search for disturbances to observe firsthand. I would have refused had I been asked. The British warship *Bulwark* that had been brought into Hong Kong to signal determination to stand against rioters would not have protected me, and nobody was offering a police escort. What could I have learned from another foray into trouble that would have been useful to the US government? The crowds would reveal nothing about the intentions of the major players in the crisis.

True to Emrys Davies' word, the HKG set out methodically to get the vitriolic posters off the streets. It wasn't long before the police met with resistance. Leftist unions had a strong presence in transportation and public utilities. When police were attacked in several areas, there were injuries, hundreds of arrests and several deaths in mid-June.

The leftist press screamed police brutality. The Struggle Committee and communist unions called for strikes. Although sporadic, the stoppages often disrupted transport and utilities, and also affected some government offices. The government responded by firing workers who did not return to work. The Struggle Committee promised financial support to the sacked workers, but overreached. With thousands of strikers being fired, that promise was unsustainable. Ultimately it could not deliver.

There were renewed calls for general strikes for the last week of June, throughout industry, public services, and government offices. Transportation, where the leftist unions were the strongest, was severely affected as large numbers of bus, tram and ferry workers didn't report for work. The leftists were also able to bring food supplies from China to a virtual halt for several days, causing shortages and much higher prices in those markets that did not participate in the strike. The Hong Kong government claimed that there was no intent by China to halt the food supplies; that it was the striking local drivers who refused to transport the food from the border. I had no contradictory information. After four days, on July 2 that strike abruptly ended, with communist newspapers proclaiming triumph of the patriotic left.

Much of the population faced serious obstacles buying food and getting to work. Transport was so disrupted that the government had to truck civil servants to their offices. Other workers who needed to cross the harbor or use buses or trams encountered long delays or no service at all. I personally felt no inconvenience from these strikes, because we didn't depend on public transportation, nor did we venture into crowded areas.

The so-called general strikes came to an end after only a few days. It soon became clear that communist calls for endless struggle had come face to face with mass firing of employees who didn't show up for work. Allen Whiting and I wondered about the leftists' ability to sustain large scale strikes once it became clear that striking workers would lose their livelihoods.

The government propaganda effort capitalized on complaints about the disruptions, gradually gaining the upper hand in the battle of words. With widespread disruptions of public services now totally divorced from labor issues, there was a rapid loss of sympathy for the left. A public that saw workers' grievances as justified and the government as anti-labor was rapidly evolving to resentment of Maoist excesses that disrupted daily lives. Apathetic acceptance of a callous colonial regime was becoming support for law and order, and even respect for police efforts to maintain it. The public was showing willingness to tolerate a degree of police brutality if that's what it took to restore tranquility.

My reporting suggested that with public opinion turning to disgust at leftist excesses, the general strikes were a strategic mistake. But calling a halt to the strikes and proclaiming victory didn't mean that challenges to authority were winding down. Hardly a week went by without another scare about China's support for pressing on with the "patriotic struggle."

CHAPTER 36

Life Without Water

DURING FALL, WINTER and spring's drier months, Hong Kong's reservoirs were unable to provide sufficient water for its residents and factories. The colony had a contract with the Kwangtung authorities to make up for the shortfall in the local supply, but did not contract for Chinese water in summer. Hong Kong usually got enough rainfall to make it until a typhoon replenished the colony's stressed reservoir system. When supply ran short, China had been a reliable provider on a spot-sale basis outside of the contract when asked.

Until China turned off the tap.

People I talked to feared that the cut-off was deliberately aimed to put pressure on Hong Kong, but the annual Dongjiang-Sham Chun Water Supply Scheme contract had been scrupulously fulfilled until its end date. Although additional water was not provided after that, there was no obligation to do so. The plausible explanation was that nobody running that regional supply scheme would dare to appear generous while Peking was calling for struggle.

The cutoff prompted strict water rationing: four hours supply to residences every four days. There were reports that many areas of the city got much less. Factories were not seriously affected. Though they consumed about seventy percent of Hong Kong's water in normal times, the export industries that were the drivers of the economy had to be kept going.

A new industry sprung up overnight. Workshops turned their talents to fashioning aluminum barrels. Everybody who could afford it scrambled for them as production ramped up to meet demand. Wealthy families could store as much water as they wanted. The poor majority had to rely on whatever utensils they had. Fortunately, precious fresh water wasn't needed to flush toilets. Hong Kong had used seawater for years, in a separate plumbing system.

Kam-lan located an oil drum–sized barrel for us and got it delivered. When the water came on, she attached a hose to the spigot and held on for an eternity while the barrel slowly filled. Then it was fill everything else: bathtub, sinks, pots and pans. We knew it would take a lot of water to keep Ruth's bottom clean. By the time all was done, water pressure was often down to a trickle.

Our first summer in Hong Kong taught us about being drenched in sweat whenever we were outside. The temperature routinely went into the nineties, most often with humidity to match. Showers morning and evening were insufficient to keep sweat at bay from the minute we stepped out of the bathtub.

That summer of 1967 I would stare at the bathtub with envy, but none of us dared to jump in. That water was first for Ruth, then for the dishes and only later for washing our sweat-soaked clothes, rancid with the odor of body salts.

The water rationing brought back memories of navy days on that World War II Fletcher-class destroyer, chasing Russian ships in the Caribbean during the Cuba Missile crisis. We didn't have the capacity to distill enough seawater for 272 showers a day for the crew. In the stifling tropical heat we were always desperately short. "Take navy showers" was an order. Turn on the water a few seconds to get wet. Turn off the water. Soap down. Get clean. Turn on just long enough to get the soap off. Get out without wasting any more of the precious fluid.

The memory sparked a twinge of jealousy. In Hong Kong we didn't have the luxury of turning a spigot on and off for a navy shower. What we could hope for was enough remaining water to dip a washcloth in and try to get clean from there.

Barbara, Kam-lan and I learned to tolerate a great deal of sweat. We would make a barrel and a bathtub last until the water came on again. Sometimes it was late. That four-hour supply became a guessing game.

As the days wore on and the authorities in Kwangtung gave no answer to requests to buy more water the sense of unease grew. Emrys Davies told me that none of the water people on the Chinese side were even answering their phones. Public sweat about Hong Kong's future was constant, as acrid as our collective concern about how and when all this might end.

CHAPTER 37

Psych Warfare at the Border

ONE OF MY FAVORITE ACTIVITIES had been the weekend hikes out of the city with friends introduced by Thomas Hui, my assistant. Like so much else during the emergency, our excursions had come to a halt. Safety was a concern, but it probably should not have been. What we learned about minor incidents in the New Territories in May and June was that local village elders were successful in convincing potential agitators to leave their villages alone. In retrospect, it would not have been necessary to abandon a trip to the New Territories unless another wildcat strike in the city disrupted the transportation required to get there.

In any case, the riots kept me too busy in the office on the weekends to think about hiking. Events had to be reported. I needed to clear the pile of miscellaneous paper and reporting that I had not been able to get to during the week. Saturdays and Sundays were when I could be found trying to learn about events in China, particularly how they might affect Hong Kong. The Political Section reporting was all about chaos. Nobody could be sure who was in charge in Peking, and turmoil in the provinces was at least as difficult to fathom. It seemed plausible that the PRC threats to the Hong Kong government came not from established leaders like Chou En-lai, but from radical factions challenging them. Burt Levin and Bill Wells educated me on that score.

Some days were calmer than others. During such a hiatus, Emrys Davies offered a trip up to the border. "Just so you will understand what it's like," he said.

"Is it safe?"

"As long as the Chinese want to keep it that way."

I eagerly accepted the offer to see for myself the restricted zone that buffered the New Territories from the Sham Chun River border. Emrys arranged for a British Army major to be my escort. When introduced he said little more than a prisoner of war might have. He had been serving with the regiment assigned to the forward defense of Hong Kong for the past two years. We would visit Lo Wu. I would stay by his side.

The regiment provided an older car that lacked air conditioning, testimony in muggy Hong Kong to the British reputation for keeping a stiff upper lip no matter what. We proceeded along a narrow road shared by trucks that straightened out the curves and belched diesel exhaust with belligerent flatulence. We took it in the face until we could take no more, then closed the windows and sweated buckets waiting for a chance to open the windows for a few seconds until the next smoky truck forced us to the narrow shoulder where we gasped and closed the windows again.

By the time we descended from the hills I felt like a chimney sweep just coming off the job. After our struggle with the trucks, the rice shoots close to harvest waving in the breeze projected an air of tranquility that was totally out of synch with the traffic we had just encountered. We took the road adjacent to the restricted area that ran east-west about a mile south of the border. I looked out across the sea of paddy fields stretching from the Hong Kong side all the way to mountains visible in the distance, but could not see the river that divided us from China. "The river is no barrier," said the major, "but the Chinese devote considerable effort to insuring that people seeking refuge in Hong Kong cannot cross it."

I never could have imagined that the fields I saw then would become host to more than ten million people in Shenzhen, China's first special economic zone. Now that landscape is filled with skyscrapers and factories, the descendants of the sweatshops that once were the hallmark of Hong Kong's economy and the cradle of the 1967 riots. A few decades later, manufacturing moved out of Hong Kong to Shenzhen en masse. Now the workers in the special economic zone strive for better conditions, like the Hong Kong workers did fifty years ago, while the emissions from Shenzhen factories foul the air of Hong Kong and the surrounding areas in China.

We approached the Lo Wu border crossing and parked by the small cement building that was the British border station. Just beyond it were the railway tracks, a platform and a narrow bridge for foot traffic. It wasn't until I was inside the building and looked out a window that I could see the stream that separated the tiny British colony from the vastness of China. I doubt that it was more than ten yards wide.

My escort suggested that we take a stroll along the footpath on our side of the river, as casually as if we were on a garden path alongside a stream in a nineteenth-century painting of the English countryside. "You'll get a good look at how the PLA mans the other side. Everyone seems to be watched by someone standing right by him, as if to make sure that nobody makes a run for it."

I could feel the suspicion in the eyes following us as we stepped outside the building. We looked at the guards. They looked at us. Another few yards down the path a soldier on the other side of the stream stared harder, moved his arms with deliberate care, and trained a machine-gun on us.

I stiffened. "Don't worry," said the major. "They do that all the time to test us. Psych warfare. We instruct our guards not to show any reaction, and not to point any weapons in their direction."

A stream of sweat trickled down my back as I contemplated the possibility of a Red Guard welcome with a volley of machine-gun fire. "Just keep walking." The major seemed more relaxed than he had been in the car, in his element. I wasn't excited about becoming a victim of my effort to match his stiff upper lip. The machine-gun tracked us. Then I followed instructions and didn't look back. There was no place to run.

I was so pissed off I couldn't stop shaking. Fuckers. A senseless mob had already taught me the chill fear of death. That son of a bitch on the other side of the stream could pull the trigger by accident, or not by accident. A metallic taste of bullets was on my tongue. Fuck the major too, for his stiff upper lip. Is it a crime to piss in your pants when you stare an untimely death in the face? I pressed hard on my crotch to hold it in, but not before a dribble left a little spot on my trousers.

Then we chatted, me and the major. "The Chinese do the border security work. There are only a few British troops stationed here, more a symbolic presence than one that would be effective if the Chinese decided to let their refugees escape to Hong Kong. Every so often they loosen up and that's when we see people coming across. They're the lucky ones. Normally they have to swim across the bay. They bet their lives on basketballs to keep them afloat. They don't really know how to swim. Many drown trying."

As we walked back, that soldier on the other side trained his machine-gun on us again. "Let's look him straight in the eye," said my escort. I wondered whether we might be denied the opportunity to blink first. The soldier, stiff, grim-faced, stared back. We picked up the pace a bit. Somehow I held my piss better the second time as we made it back to the guardhouse.

"The men here get used to it," said the major. "It gets a little tense, but there's no indication that anything serious will happen. If it does, there's little we can do about it."

I called Emrys to thank him for arranging the tour.

Emrys spoke calmly, but I could feel the force in his voice. "Now you have seen it for yourself. Man for man the Gurkha regiment that backs up our troops on the border is the toughest fighting force in the world, but there is no way they could stop a concerted Chinese attempt to take over. The People's Liberation Army could wade across that river," he said. "If they really want Hong Kong, we'll leave. They can have it."

CHAPTER 38

Senior Staff Meetings

I REPORTED ON MY LO WU visit in the weekly senior staff meeting, surmising that it felt tense at times, but there was no indication that the Chinese were planning to storm across the border. Then I choked, realizing how dumb I was to say that when there was so much going on in China that I didn't know about.

Junior diplomats have to be careful with their language, particularly when they are in the presence of far more senior people. Saving myself from idiocy didn't come easy. I confessed that nothing I had seen told me anything about China's ultimate intentions toward Hong Kong. All I had to go on was the British major's comment that there was nothing unusual going on at the border.

My inclusion in these meetings after the May riots came as a surprise. Normally such gatherings were exclusive, convened by the chief of mission and his deputy for section chiefs who listened, reported, and later conveyed what they would to staffers. I certainly did not have the personal rank to be included. The Hong Kong/Macau "political section" was not a section at all, but a single FSO included in the

Economic Section—until Allen Whiting separated me from subservience to Lynn Olson.

Consul General Rice had decided to expand these weekly staff meetings to more than forty people as it became clear there was intense interest in what was engulfing China. Now, with Cultural Revolution–inspired demonstrators marching right past our building up Garden Road to Government House, the need for everybody to know what was going on in Hong Kong was also urgent.

I was brought in as the cub reporter charged with summarizing the week's developments in the streets and answering questions. Were we really in danger? Would Hong Kong survive intact under British rule? When would the disturbances end?

Richard Nethercutt spoke first. He was clean cut and studious, the modest chief of the five-man Mainland Political Section who was too nice a person to get promoted to the top ranks of the Foreign Service. We listened intently as he summed up what his section had learned about China's convulsions during the past week, sharing travelers' tales and horror stories from various sources. He spoke of huge demonstrations and big-character posters denouncing as capitalist roaders leaders who had devoted their lives to Mao.

All the information the Political Section could gather suggested that marauding gangs of Red Guards were bringing about the collapse of order wherever they went. Mao's call for perpetual revolution meant that anyone could become a target, no matter how respected they had been just weeks or days before.

The Red Guards attacked established authorities, invaded homes and smashed whatever relics of 5,000 years of Chinese culture they could find. Not content just to humiliate anyone they called bourgeois, they seemed intent on destroying the ability to govern, and they were beyond Mao's control. Meanwhile, Mao's wife Chiang Ching and her Gang of Four appeared determined to keep the loyal cadre in fear of their positions, if not their lives.

My turn came next. I looked around the room as I gathered my thoughts and fended off panic. Besides Messrs. Rice, Whiting, Nethercutt and Olson, there was Mr. Farnsworth, Sandy Marlowe from USIA, and a long forgotten administrative officer. I had met the FBI representative, and the Science, Military and Commercial Liaison Officers, but there were quite a few others I did not know. I just assumed they were CIA or other intelligence officers.

I didn't have time to think about being the youngest and most inexperienced person in these staff meetings. I was not yet twenty-nine, a first-tour FSO to be exposed to the various sections for about six months each to acquaint me with the Foreign Service. Now I was on center stage at staff meetings, briefing people who hungered for far more information than they could get from the *South China Morning Post.*

Were the Hong Kong Red Guard copycats targeting Westerners in more violent ways than calling them white-skinned pigs? Are the underpaid Chinese front-line police staying loyal to the colonial government? How many deaths and injuries? Would the demonstrators try to take over government buildings? What parts of town were relatively safe, and what should be avoided? Will Hong

Kong make it through the summer without having to impose even stricter water rationing than what's already in place? What are China's ultimate intentions?

I had no way of divining Chinese intentions, other than weighing PRC propaganda against the views of the people I talked to. Among the most perceptive were CIA Station Chief Bill Wells, Emrys Davies, Maynard Parker, and my friend in the Political Section, Burt Levin. All opined that Peking was really crazy if they were serious about taking Hong Kong back. That complicated the analysis. Allen Whiting was as perceptive as anybody, but usually I was given the benefit of his views only after I brought him my draft reports.

I followed Whiting's advice, and expressed optimism that the Hong Kong government would survive the communist challenge. I believed that, because Peking's threats were becoming vaguer as the local leftists were showing less ability to organize mass protests. The public was turning against them. But what we could not be sure of was the intentions of the Chinese government, itself convulsed by the Cultural Revolution.

No doubt I had more confidence than knowledge, but that was a good thing. Otherwise I would have been too terrified to speak. Somehow I did what I was supposed to do in front of all those senior people. I summed up events and conceded that I wasn't one who could know PRC intentions. Perhaps I was learning the diplomatic art of hedging one's bets.

Somebody on the far side of the room who I did not recognize asked a question that must have been on everybody's minds. "Will the Chinese authorities in Kwangtung resume supplying water when contract renewal time comes up on October 1?"

I couldn't answer that question.

I suspected that quite a few people at these meetings were CIA, because they never said anything. Even Wild Bill Wells, affable and loquacious in private, had very little to say in this forum. He must have found it convenient to leave the talking to Nethercutt and me, as long as I didn't say anything to suggest that the information came from sensitive CIA sources.

Mr. Olson also said very little at these meetings. My neutered boss should have had valuable information to report about how the Hong Kong economy was performing under the stress of the disturbances. Perhaps he was fuming in silence over all the attention I was getting. His scowl suggested that he had never enjoyed such status in his long career. I confess that I wasn't sensitive to how much Whiting's decision to make a star out of me had humiliated him. I was too naïve and self-centered to even think about it.

CHAPTER 39

Precious Treasures

EVERY SO OFTEN I WAS ABLE to get out of the office and wander around the Central District. I loved to browse antiques, and plenty were coming out of China. The shops were a feast for the eyes and profound sadness for the heart. The Red Guards forced people to watch as they destroyed family heirlooms, precious art, porcelains, and ivory carvings, even the *shen dzwo* prayer tables for ancestor worship. Pillage was personal and public. People gave away their treasures if there was hope of saving them from the rampage. Antique stores in Hong Kong filled up with refugee treasures that were snuck out of China.

During the height of the crisis, Chinese antiques and art were on sale for a pittance, because the Hong Kong dealers were as nervous as the bulk of the population. Several of them told me that they feared that their stores would become targets of local mobs intending to emulate the Red Guards. A chat with the proprietor of Yue Po Chai Antiques was a useful barometer of apprehension that China intended to make the Pearl of the Orient uninhabitable under British rule.

Unlike Lane Crawford, the iconic British department store and oasis for expats, the articles for sale at Yue Po Chai up on Hollywood Road by the Man Mo Temple and Cat Street were not marked with prices, only a little sticker with a code for the benefit of the seller. Hong Kong was a place where you bargained for almost everything of value. I came to believe that a comparison of the asking price for antiques and what they actually sold for was a rough measure of fear that all would be lost during the Cultural Revolution.

I really wanted to find something memorable to celebrate my survival that May 11, when I was caught in the mob. At Yue Po Chai I gingerly slithered between display stands competing for space to promote their porcelains, ivory, jade, and coral carvings. Hanging scrolls intruded on each other's space along the walls.

I spotted a most unusual ivory carving. The bottom part was a low-cut bowl about five inches in diameter and two inches high, topped by an eight-inch chimney. The shape was similar to a North China traditional hot pot where you dip your little basket of morsels into a steaming moat of very hot broth that circles the flue.

Mrs. Yue came over and gushed, "You know real treasure." She sat me down at a table and offered a cup of tea. Exquisite aroma, delicate taste. She turned the piece in her hand with the grace of an artist, pointing out the delicate feathers of the phoenix, the power of the dragon encircling her on the flue, the intricate lattice carved into the bowl. "A treasure carved for the Ching Emperor Ch'ien-lung," she said, but only after telling me that I spoke wonderful Cantonese. I politely denied the praise.

"And what does it cost?" I ask.

"Ah, you have to understand its magnificence. I give you special price. For a Ch'ien-lung piece, price almost nothing."

I asked again and still was given no idea how much she would ask for this masterpiece. I turned the piece upside down, revealing four characters carved into the base. They could either be authentic or faked identification of the emperor for whom it was carved and year of his reign. It didn't matter. To this day I have never seen another carving like it.

I turned the vase around gingerly and ran my fingers over the intricate details of the mythical bird and dragon that symbolized the emperor and empress, the embodiment of male and female. Mrs. Yue excused herself to hover over another customer. When she returned I asked the price again.

"Any emperor would love this piece. It unique." She extolled its singular virtues again, and a third time. Price was the last item on her list of things to discuss. By the time it was revealed, I had heard an elaborate story about people braving great danger to smuggle art works out of China to save them from destruction at the hands of ravaging Red Guards. "We are so lucky this treasure escaped destruction. You steal it for only US$200."

"My oh my. Much too expensive." I had to say this in such a way that it would be taken as slightly derisive and also as a joke. Genuine insults killed deals. This "You must be kidding" phase in the negotiation must be handled delicately.

"Such a treasure. I sell you much too cheap. Give you such great bargain because you speak wonderful Cantonese. Better than any foreigner."

"Polite talk. You know that's not so. This is a nice piece, but there are so many fakes now. I don't know. . . ."

"Not fake." Offense was written in a deep frown. "I charge you much too little for precious art. Maybe I charge more you appreciate better." She paused for a moment, but hardly long enough to allow me time to reply. "What you want to pay?" The get-serious bargaining smile returned to her face.

I offered her US$70. No doubt I was on that border of insult that killed negotiations.

"You say $700." She smiled. "I could accept HK$700, special for you."

"That's not what I said," sure she knew.

Mrs. Yue was a master at keeping the negotiation going. I knew people were afraid to buy. Rumors were flying that the Red Guards, and maybe even the People's Liberation Army were preparing to smash the Pearl of the Orient.

She pressed ahead. "Seven hundred Hong Kong very special price, much less than before."

Confuse the customer. HK$700 was about $115 in US currency.

The talk about bargaining was that even foreigners were supposed to be able to buy China's treasures for half or less than the offering price. The challenge was to pay just enough to win the purchase and earn the respect of the seller, while paying a decent price for both sides and giving each side face.

This dance over the ivory vase went on for more than an hour until I said that $500 Hong Kong was really all I could afford to pay, US$83.

There was silence. I really wanted to buy this extraordinary tribute to my time in Hong Kong.

Mrs. Yue's exasperation was clear on her face. "$510 or no deal." There was a hint of a sword in her voice.

This was a piece of historic art that I could admire for a lifetime. My Ruth Leslie would pass it on too, with stories of where she was born and how her father acquired it.

That was the drop-dead price. I was not the barbarian fool tourist who accepted the first offer, and I should not be the prideful fool who rejected the last.

In 1988 two curators from the National Palace Museum in Taipei examined my treasure. They were quite certain that this ivory carving was an authentic work which would bring a substantial sum on the international art market. I would never sell it.

Every so often I think that had I taken every penny I had and bought what I could of the treasures that escaped the Cultural Revolution and made their way to Hong Kong during the 1967 disturbances, I would have a small museum of survivors of a culture of extraordinary beauty to share with my descendants.

No time for regret now. The sharing will be mostly in the form of this book of memories.

CHAPTER 40

Attack Across the Border

IT SEEMS THAT EVERY LULL in the 1967 Hong Kong disturbances was mere prelude to an even more shocking incident.

Sha Tau Kok was an unusual village. Half of it was on the Chinese side of the border. We did not visit there during my tour. Had I known about its divided status, I would have wanted to see how that section of the border was controlled. Such was my ignorance of the Frontier Closed Area that I knew only that there was a restricted buffer zone along the entire border to control immigration, and that some farmers tilled fields on both sides of the border.

Sha Tau Kok exploded into Hong Kong headlines on July 8. There is no agreed version of exactly what happened, but I prefer the Hong Kong government version over the claims put forth by the *People's Daily*. The government maintained that a well-organized group of 300–400 people from the Chinese side crossed the border late in the morning and surrounded the police post situated about fifty yards on the Hong Kong side. The crowd threw homemade bombs over the station's perimeter fence. The police fired tear gas and baton shells in an attempt to disperse the crowd. Then machine-gun fire erupted from across the border.

The post was attacked again in mid-afternoon, with bullets from the Chinese side and more homemade bombs. Five policemen were killed by gunfire and another eleven were wounded. Such an attack from China was unprecedented in Hong Kong's colonial history.

I did not have access to 24/7 reporting of the incident, but next morning Thomas Hui gave me his translation of a report in the pro-Peking *Hong Kong Evening News,* which stated that Chinese militia had crossed the border. I would learn later from Burt Levin that at HKG urging, the British chargé in Peking was lodging a protest while I was reading about the incident in the local papers. The Chinese vice foreign minister preempted the chargé's protest, accusing the border police of firing first and demanding a public apology and punishment of the culprits.

The *People's Daily* version alleged that residents on the Hong Kong side of the border had joined a rally on the Chinese side to "support the patriotic struggle against British persecution." Peking's mouthpiece accused the border police of attacking these residents when they returned to the Hong Kong side, and of ignoring warning shots before the Chinese responded. The report accused the Hong Kong police of killing one demonstrator and wounding others, which was the only fact agreed on by both sides.

News of the Chinese attack and the police deaths spread quickly through Hong Kong, and with it pervasive fear that this could be a harbinger of more troop incursions. Fear of a Chinese takeover was endemic. The reports of heavy machine-gun fire spurred widespread rumors of PLA involvement. At the very least, the Chinese army contingent in the area stood by and did nothing to restrain what looked like a well-planned incident by local authorities.

The HKG replaced the border police with troops from the British Garrison. Up until that time, the only British troops stationed on the border were those at the Lo Wu railway checkpoint, where I had visited. This did nothing to reduce the jitters throughout Hong Kong, where increasing numbers of people who could do so were looking for a way out. Having the Gurkha regiment on backup near the border only underlined the fragility of Hong Kong's defenses.

The Sha Tau Kok incident, and the way it was played by the Chinese Foreign Ministry and the *People's Daily* were trumpeted in Hong Kong's communist press as PRC endorsement of armed support for the confrontation. In the days that followed there were demonstrations in several areas of Hong Kong and attacks on police who came to disperse them. Buses were set on fire as the Struggle Committee promised guerrilla warfare. It was easy to believe that the Sha Tau Kok incident and the incitement that followed inspired the upsurge in violence. But it was hardly a mass outpouring of rage. Rather it was the work of small groups that carried on the challenges to Hong Kong authority and spread fear much more widely than their numbers would suggest.

I shuddered when I finished writing up this report. After what happened at Sha Tau Kok, it looked like my visit to the border was on a very lucky day.

CHAPTER 41

Impeccable Agent

I LAMENTED MY MISPLACED OPTIMISM that the situation seemed to be calming down after the communists had called an end to the food strike only a week before. As the tension grew, so did my anxiety to talk to Y.C. Liang. At one of our frequent meetings in the front office Wild Bill Wells offered him up as a person to speak to in critical times.

"He'll probably talk to you because you speak Cantonese." I got the impression that Wells might have been working to establish this contact for me for some time.

I knew little about Y.C. Liang. He was the head of the gold syndicate in Macau and a very wealthy entrepreneur involved in many businesses in Hong Kong as well as the nominally Portuguese colony. Wells told me that he was unusually well connected, likely to be the best source we could have on both local and Mainland Chinese communist intentions.

Mr. Liang's secretary returned Wells' call and gave a time for me to visit at 1 Po Shan Road. The drive there offered stunning views of Kowloon from the narrow lane that had been cut out of the steep hillside. I weaved between the precipice overlooks and lush tropical growth, finally arriving at a stately manor standing serenely by itself, overlooking the teeming city of almost four million crowded souls. Beyond the solitary splendor, skyscrapers stood on stilts balanced on precipices, pointing toward the harbor, Kowloon, and mountains in the distance. Though I grew up with views of the Manhattan skyline, nothing was quite so dramatic as gazing at Hong Kong from the grandeur of Y.C. Liang's mansion.

A servant dressed in white livery opened the door and led me to a drawing room where Y.C. bid me to sit opposite him in a Victorian armchair that might have been a museum piece. A second servant brought in tea in traditional cups without handles, serving me, then Y.C. We sipped, silent. I blew into the cup surreptitiously so I wouldn't scorch my flute-sensitive tongue. I wasn't playing the flute much during the crisis, but my tongue never lost its propensity for being scalded by hot beverages.

Y.C. apologized profusely for the delay in arranging the appointment. I blushed, asking myself what it must take to appear so deferential when the gulf between us in accomplishment, prestige and wealth was wider than the ocean that separated the continents where we were born.

"I had important business in Macau and China," he explained.

We, meaning the CIA, knew that Liang had been a very important go-between for both Macau and Hong Kong in their dealings with the PRC leaders in Kwangtung and Peking. He had connections on all sides dating back twenty-five years or more to World War II. He was considered to be more than discreet—virtually anonymous. As for his connection with our CIA, I doubted that he would have been a paid agent. One look at his opulent residence, with its luxury European interior decoration and furniture made it abundantly clear that he had no need for the money.

Mr. Liang was stately in a traditional black gown like those worn during formal occasions or in austere family portraits. He looked like the model for a scholar in a brush painting. His placid expression gave no hint of what might be behind it, save for seeming to be perfectly at ease. I was not.

He looked me over carefully. Unlike almost every other Chinese I had met, he did not open the conversation with empty compliments about my language ability. Instead, he asked how I had learned Cantonese. I told him about my one-on-one repeat-after-me classes for six months, and asked if he would bear with my limitations and forgive me when I needed to ask him to repeat something or explain until I could understand it. While I was fairly confident of my ability to express my own ideas, I could not pretend to understand all of the five or ten different ways that a native speaker might express the same thought. Mr. Liang said I should call him Y.C., the Romanized initials of his given name, Yun-chang. I was told he spoke reasonably good English, but he did not use it with me.

I had been advised early on by Lung Sing not to start off a conversation by asking political questions like reporters did. "Sit and listen until people signal readiness to talk about what you want to hear." I also knew that I couldn't ask Y.C. how he came to know Bill Wells, or why he was willing to see me to talk about the communists' real intentions toward Hong Kong.

Y.C. offered that he had met quite a few British and some Americans over the years. He told me a bit about his adventures during World War II. "You know the Japanese did not occupy Macau," he said, "so it was a haven for agents of all kinds, the British, the Japanese, the Americans even." He told me that he had worked very closely with the British and had also been involved in getting downed American pilots to safety. "I was proud to help the Allies during the War with the Japanese. The British offered me an O.B.E. It was a big honor to be an Officer of the British Empire, but I had to turn it down." Accepting it would have labeled him as a lackey of London and ended his role as a go-between despite his extensive contacts with the communists.

There were many things that Y.C. did not tell me. According to Philip Snow's *The Fall of Hong Kong*, "Y.C. Liang, then a young businessman who worked as comprador for the local firm of Wong Tai, was the true linchpin of British resistance. Code-named Phoenix, he organized the escape routes for the Allies from Macau to Free China, and the arteries for British intelligence work. Some of Phoenix's exploits were mildly spectacular. On one occasion he brought about the deliberate flooding of some bank vaults where he knew vital radio valves to be stored. Handymen in his pay were called in to pump out the water—and took the opportunity to secure the valves.

When the Japanese surrendered, London desperately needed to send a message to Franklin Gimson, the colonial secretary who had been interned by the Japanese, instructing him to re-establish a British civil administration in Hong Kong, and to get in first and do it before any Chinese or American administration was formed. Y.C. was entrusted with delivering the message."

In Snow's account, a young Chinese aged about thirty and "immaculately dressed in a white silk robe appeared on August 23, 1945 like an angel out of the Gospels. It was Phoenix, the British Army Aid Group agent newly arrived in Hong Kong, who had also been assigned the additional task of prompting local initiative. And after a day or two, during which Phoenix made his appearance with the formal orders from Whitehall, Gimson took on the role of acting governor and led his colleagues out of Stanley to set up his long-planned skeleton government in the heart of Victoria [Central District], in the former French Mission building."

Now, twenty-two years later, Y.C. patiently explained to me how Mao Tse-tung's wife Chiang Ching and her Gang of Four had terrified even the top tier leadership closest to the Chairman. "Chou En-lai remains in place as the voice of sanity but often has to pander to the radicals who are intent on purging the leaders and taking their place. The survivors of the purges are trying to run the country, but Chiang Ching and her followers are running riot. Power struggles are erupting everywhere. The Foreign Ministry demand for an apology after Sha Tau Kok shows how strong the radicals are in this time of turmoil and confusion. Any effort to bring them under control invites accusations of betraying the Cultural Revolution.

"The disturbances will go on for some time. There will be more violent incidents. For now, the leaders who want to calm things down cannot afford the risk of denunciation and purge if they appear to be siding with the British. What can be hoped for is less propaganda urging Hong Kong comrades to struggle against imperialism until they smash it . . ." he hesitated for a moment, "but I think even that will take time."

Y.C. agreed when I said I didn't think the leftists had support beyond the communist-controlled unions and their other organizations in Hong Kong. Despite major labor grievances, the city was built on the voluntary sweat of those who had fled chaos, starvation, or poverty much more extreme than found in the colony. There was little taste for destroying stability except among the band of zealots who took to the streets when called upon to struggle.

Y.C. told me that the leadership of Beijing's New China News Agency was the guiding force behind the riots, not the All Circles Struggle Committee, but in recent days coordination seemed to be slipping out of control as small bands acted on their own.

I asked how and when the disturbances might end. He mulled over this for a moment. "Nobody knows when they will end, but they will die down as workers realize that nobody will support them if they are fired for going on strike. If the moderates regain more control in Beijing, their appointees in Hong Kong will follow."

I thanked Y.C. for being so helpful, clasping my hands in an expression of gratitude. As Bill Wells had told me, he would be an incredibly useful source if he trusted me. I think he did.

I cannot help but wonder if Y.C. Liang wasn't also a key advisor to Governor Sir David Trench. When the crisis was over, Y.C. invited me to a dinner he hosted for more than a hundred people in his home, in honor of the governor. The meal was quite extraordinary, the most memorable of more Chinese banquets than I can count. Every dish was snake.

CHAPTER 42

Incipient Civil War

Y.C. GAVE ME A LOT TO REPORT. His appraisal sounded like it might have come directly from Premier Chou En-lai in Peking and the Mainland appointed leaders of the New China News Agency in Hong Kong. I wrote up his part of the conversation verbatim, translating from the remembered Cantonese into idiomatic English as I scribbled on a lined yellow pad. Allen Whiting was pleased. The outgoing message identified the source only as a well-connected businessman. We shared the CIA's concern about protecting important sources, and that often meant not trusting our colleagues in Washington to keep a secret.

That didn't mean I wasn't going to share what I learned with Burt Levin. He in turn briefed me on more chaos in China. We focused on Y.C.'s comments about the power and influence of the radicals in Peking, and how it meant nobody could openly take a position that it was time to halt efforts to destabilize Hong Kong. The risks of losing one's head were much too high. As Y.C. suggested, that evolution would take time.

July was turning out to be the most tumultuous period so far in the Cultural Revolution convulsions. "There's no telling who is in power where," said Burt. "It's a guessing game as to who in the provinces are loyal to which group in Peking."

By the end of the month incipient civil war was lurking in parts of China. A cable to State reported that, "Both the *People's Daily* and Peking Radio earlier today warned local authorities in Wuhan to surrender or face destruction by the Chinese Army. The interesting thing is that none of our sophisticated intelligence gathering means have given any indication that the Army is planning to do anything of the sort." This report, dated July 26, 1967, asserted that "there is a rising tide of reports from all over the country indicating that the disorder is getting worse. . . . If Peking is unable to bring this situation under control, other local authorities will decide that it is safe to be defiant, and that could mean the beginning of the end for the Mao-Lin combine." Such was our understanding of developments in China as the Hong Kong communists pressed on for more violence in the days after the Sha Tau Kok incident.

CHAPTER 43

Climactic Crackdown

IN HONG KONG, THE UPSURGE in incidents after Sha Tau Kok led quickly to a change in government strategy. Emrys Davies gave me a heads up. "Instead of responding defensively to poster-pasters, demonstrators and vandalism, we will be raiding local communist organizations' headquarters." Within days the police went after the more powerful unions like Transport and the Dock Workers, which had been prominent in the strikes.

Emergency regulations permitted searches of suspect premises without warrants and detention without trial. Other regulations prohibited the possession of virtually anything that could be used as an offensive weapon. Along with the raids, the police went after prominent leftists. The Struggle Committee had named its members, providing a convenient target list. Police had a trove of photographic evidence of leadership in the riots and demonstrations. Left-wing union leaders were picked up during raids on their premises.

There is no doubt that the emergency regulations amounted to a complete suspension of basic civil rights designed to give the police and the government the power to do whatever they thought necessary to suppress the challenge. Weak voices regretting the suspension of the rule of law were drowned out by events: the firebombing of a police station, a policeman killed by demonstrators, calls to continue the struggle until final victory, and an increasing number of crude bombs. For the great majority of Hong Kong residents, yearning for safe streets easily prevailed over concerns for the legal niceties of civil rights. Thomas Hui told me he was absolutely certain of that.

I didn't keep count of the number of police raids in July and the first days of August, but it certainly was in the dozens. The leftist press claimed sixty, said Thomas, with at least 1,500 arrests and five deaths.

Yet the spate of bombs, real and fake, suggested that a hit-and-run guerrilla campaign was well underway. Though there was little damage, they caused lots of hassle, as the police had to treat the fake bombs with the same caution as the real ones. The bombs further disrupted the public transport system, already severely hampered by a shortage of drivers after the dismissal of the strikers who didn't heed the ultimatum to return to work.

As Y.C. Liang had hinted, it was not possible to say when calm might return to Hong Kong, no matter how effective the police might be in forcing leftist leaders to go underground.

It was clear that any local leftist organization could be a target, but the Hong Kong government did not touch the pillars of Peking's presence in the colony, the New China News Agency and the Bank of China. This despite the Bank of China's role and compelling evidence from intelligence sources that the guiding hand behind the challenge to British authority was the New China News Agency.

The logic behind leaving key Peking-owned institutions alone was simple. With Peking still voicing rhetorical support for continued struggle, such a direct move would almost certainly lead to great pressure in Peking for retaliatory action. In the chaos that was China, that could mean almost anything, including a serious incursion across the border to "protect the interests of the 700 million Chinese people."

With the numbing frequency of almost daily raids, arrests and incidents, I came to wonder whether my reports might not be making for boring reading in Washington. I hinted as much to Allen Whiting. "It doesn't matter. If we don't continue to send them something every day, they'll howl." I couldn't help but get the impression that State Department people were bored at their desks, hungry for tidbits of news to make their day. Perhaps Senator Magnuson would make a serious effort to get permission to go to China and the Germans would ask again if that signaled a change in policy.

I never got any feedback on my reporting. It seemed that everything to do with Washington was a one-way street—from us to them.

I don't recall ever being bored myself. There was too much to do just to keep track and report, too much encouragement and banter with Whiting, and then the thoughtful exchanges with Bill Wells, Burt Levin, and a whole host of reporters and scholars who were frequent visitors to the office. I would be concealing the truth if I didn't admit to feeling puffed up by the position, reveling in my prominence at the weekly staff meetings and in the knowledge that I was considered by important people to be a valuable source of information for their newspapers, wire services, and academic research.

The ongoing raids on leftist organizations came to a spectacular climax on August 4. A combined operation numbering approximately 1,000 policemen and British Army soldiers raided a building in North Point that housed leftist union offices, a Chinese Products Emporium and the residences of employees of China-funded companies. Newspaper reports the next morning treated readers to big front-page photos of helicopters landing troops and police on the roof in a major military operation. Most amazing of all was the discovery of a well-equipped hospital and operating theater inside the building. It was a public relations coup, encouraging a battle-fatigued populace.

Getting together with Maynard Parker and Sydney Liu for a sumptuous *Newsweek* lunch after major developments had become a habit. "This is the real thing. The government is finally getting serious," mused Maynard.

"How do you think Peking might respond?" I asked.

"There's no telling," said Sydney Liu."

CHAPTER 44

Family Dynamic

THERE WERE TRANQUIL MOMENTS amidst the Hong Kong crisis: putting my arms around Ruth Leslie, holding a bottle to her tiny mouth and hearing her suckle, tucking my precious two-month-old into the baby carriage. On Sunday evening walks Barbara and I took turns wheeling the joy down the driveway to Coombe Road and on to Wan Chai Gap Park.

Coombe Road was a quiet street lush with semi-tropical greenery that camouflaged the homes and small apartment buildings set far apart from each other on our side of the street. While the Carolina Gardens apartment block was visible across from our flat, the complex was set deep enough off the road that my occasional attempts to peer into other people's lives were completely futile. It was easier to imagine the lights in the windows as stars in the night sky.

There was almost no vehicle traffic to interrupt the serenity. No noise but the wind as we strolled in a sea of calm.

At the end of Coombe Road was the park, an empty grassy field where people walked their dogs. From there you could see the houses in the distance, up on Mount Cameron Road. We could have been in a quiet enclave in the hills north of Los Angeles. It was all but impossible to relate our haven of lush greenery to the teeming resettlement estates and stacked tenements that most Hongkongers endured.

Before the disturbances, we had taken Shu-shu out for short walks down Coombe Road in the evenings. He was still blind in one eye and uncertain on his feet, stumbling often. As his recovery progressed, we allowed him out on his own, confident he would stay very close to home. But one day he went off and disappeared. We never found any trace of him. The loss of Shu-shu after Barbara had given this lovely dog so much intimate tender care left her grieving deeply, while I was too engrossed in my job to mourn.

As a young mother nursing a baby in this refuge above the turbulent city, Barbara lived in a quiet world. I knew that she missed our dog terribly, but she seemed otherwise secure and very close to Ruth. I was too much in the vortex of Hong Kong's struggle to be a real part of her universe. She allowed me those quiet moments when we strolled together. We rarely spoke about my job and even less about her concerns.

I didn't realize how exasperating my work habits must have been to her, until one evening I came home without my house key. I rang the doorbell, and there was no answer. I rang again, and then again for a longer time before she opened the door a few inches and slammed it in my face without a word.

I had interrupted her Cantonese lesson. Numb, I waited outside for several minutes until the teacher opened the door and slinked by me. By the time I came in, Barbara had already gone to the bedroom. As with so many other small or not so small inconsiderate acts, not a word was said about the incident afterwards. I did not question what the man might be doing in my home at nine o'clock at night. If Barbara told me beforehand that she would be hiring a Cantonese tutor, the message hadn't registered. I was too preoccupied to press her to explain this late night lesson, but I knew that I had failed again to let her know that I would not be coming home in time for dinner. That must have been what ignited her smoldering burn. I don't recall whether she continued with those at-home Cantonese lessons. Perhaps the teacher was too frightened by her burst of temper to return.

Family life in the Foreign Service suffered even in the best of circumstances. Spouses were tossed into foreign situations with precious little preparation or support while their husbands had status and plenty of work to do. Divorce rates were no lower than in the general US population, probably because ego-hyped FSOs like me paid precious little attention to their wives' real needs. Our tranquil strolls down Coombe Road were rather few, when they should have been most evenings after dinner together.

I hardly had any family life at all during the height of the crisis. By the time I got home at night I was so tired that all I was good for was watching baby Ruth gurgle for a while and having a bite of warmed-up dinner. Often enough Barbara was getting what sleep she could before

Ruth would wake her up in the middle of the night, demanding to be nursed.

Sometimes Kam-lan would stay upstairs in the apartment, watching over the crib, cleaning up in the kitchen and the living room, or warming up dinner for me. We would chat in Cantonese. She told me stories of her early life in Pok Fu Lam Village, her grandfather's riches-to-rags story during World War II, how she wished she could have continued school after sixth grade but there was no money for that. Her older brother seemed to be making decent money as a mechanic, but he didn't help her or contribute anything to the family. He wasn't really part of it anymore, not a filial son.

During these conversations I took quite a liking to Kam-lan, and it seemed as if she liked me too, but I dared not touch her. I knew that if I tried anything like that she would flee and we would never see her again.

It was not Barbara's fault that my mind sometimes strayed into thoughts of what might have been or what could be. Although my inhibitions kept curiosity and desire for other women tightly leashed, it was also true that I still hadn't gotten over the loss of Peggy Strum.

Almost seven years after I was dumped, Barbara was stuck with a huge, horribly painful void in my life that I couldn't even talk about. Always late getting home from work, almost never calling, wanting to touch my maid, curious about the intimate lives of others, still wanting to be a good husband, good father, good provider.

A biographer might conclude that the slammed door incident marked the inevitable unraveling of our marriage, a long, slow process of suppressed resentment and disappointment which hardly ever surfaced, but eventually led both of us to seek solace elsewhere and divorce twelve years later.

But in that present tense of 1967, my heady role in the consulate general on Garden Road kept me too busy to unravel the confusion.

CHAPTER 45

Burned

WHEN CHARLES MOHR CALLED UP and identified him-self as a *New York Times* foreign correspondent, I immediately welcomed him to come on by at his con-venience. My admiration for the *Times* had a long history. I have never stopped believing that it was those thirteen weeks with the News of the Week in Review that got me past the oral exam and into the Foreign Service.

Mohr was tall, balding and looking a bit rumpled in a suit that probably did not come from one of Hong Kong's renowned and ridiculously inexpensive tailors. He asked question after question.

I was eager to answer and be known as a valuable source.

He skillfully picked my brains for a detailed account of recent events. I enjoyed his intellect and his process, watch-ing him scribble furiously in a pocket-sized notebook. His special skill was keeping the conversation going all the while he was writing. I was impressed. He agreed the conversation would be off the record, no attribution to me or any American official. I trusted him.

The CIA take I had read that morning in the front office was particularly interesting, and more than normally chilling.

CHAPTER 45

The tidbit that scared me was one I probably would have shared with Maynard Parker and Sydney Liu, because we had traded so much useful information in complete confidence. I wondered if I could develop that kind of relationship with the *New York Times* and its correspondent sitting in front of me.

I asked, "Can you promise not to use certain information until you can verify it from other sources?"

"Yes, I could." Charles Mohr looked me straight in the eye. I took him at his word.

"OK. Here's something I want to know more about, and I'm sure you will too. We have a report that the Chinese have moved 8,000 PLA troops up close to the border. This must be China's response to the huge raid in North Point."

Mohr was writing in his notebook.

"You'll hold that until you learn about it elsewhere."

"Where did that come from?" he asked.

"You can figure it out. All I can say is that this information is extremely sensitive. With all that's been going on here it could cause real panic if it gets out." I didn't know where it came from, since the report only mentioned a reliable Chinese source. No point in saying that.

I was confident that our meeting, which lasted well over an hour, had established the kind of relationship where we would share what we knew with each other. My experience thus far had been that the best reporters had plenty of sources and useful information, sometimes more than I could get from my perch in the consulate general. Sharing gossip and what we learned was very useful. Charles Mohr would be equally so.

Next morning was the weekly staff meeting. I gave some thought as to what I would say. Continuing demonstrations, five deaths, including a policeman, raids and resistance with plenty of arrests and the appearance of more bombs. There would be questions about border incidents, but I couldn't say a thing about those 8,000 troops—CIA restrictions.

In other meetings, Consul General Rice had left it to Allen Whiting to start off with upcoming items that everybody needed to know about, like another CODEL visit. Not this time. The consul general glared at the assembly, and it seemed he was scowling at me a little more than at everybody else. "How did this get leaked to the press?" He read the headline aloud: "'8,000 PLA Troops Brought to the Border,'" and asked again, his glower searing my guilt.

He was livid. I was terrified. "As if there isn't enough panic in Hong Kong already," he muttered. I was choking in my own silence, fearing something worse than death if I was asked directly, and worse yet if I lied.

Consul General Rice wore thick glasses. I would never learn if he knew how terrified I was. For some reason he moved on and asked Richard Nethercutt to sum up the week's developments in Mainland China. How I got through my own report and survived the meeting was a minor miracle. I was so traumatized that I don't recall a word of what I said. Charles Mohr's betrayal and the consequences I feared were no less unforgettable than being caught in the mob on May 11. I had leaked information classified top secret. End of career.

When I got back to my office a copy of the story was on my desk. There was the headline: 8,000 PLA TROOPS

BROUGHT TO THE BORDER. I saw it. The article however does not appear in the *New York Times* archives, but may have appeared in the *International Herald Tribune,* owned by the *Times* and the *Washington Post.*

But there were two reports in the *Times* of Chinese troop movements in early August. The first states that "Chinese troop reinforcements were brought into the area near the border with Hong Kong last night to control demonstrators who several times crossed into Hong Kong territory and threw stones at British soldiers." The second reported that two regiments of PLA were moving toward Canton on August 11, but neither were the front-page story Consul General Rice had railed about.

Possibly there was fear that this story would create panic in Hong Kong and the consul general or the State Department asked the newspaper not to run it. That might also suggest that the story was watered down to the mention of Chinese troop reinforcements in the report quoted above. As both Consul General Rice and Charles Mohr passed away decades ago, I make this account without being able to definitively establish what really happened.

CHAPTER 46

Endless Jitters

I ASKED BILL WELLS WHAT he thought about the leaked report that threatened to get me in so much trouble. He smiled so broadly that I was pretty sure he had surmised that I was the one who leaked it. "It was going to get out soon enough anyway, and it could mean anything," he said. "The panic level will go up for a while, but I'm betting the PLA is there to keep the Red Guard types out of Hong Kong rather than help them come in."

There were countless rumors about PLA troops and preparations for a Chinese takeover. It mattered little whether they were wild speculation, intended to intimidate, or coming from CIA sources. They all added to pervasive feelings of uncertainty in Hong Kong.

I wondered if Emrys Davies wasn't too optimistic about the police raids driving leftist leaders underground. When Thomas Hui and I discussed what was in the pro-communist press after the spectacular raid on August 4, I couldn't help but feel that whatever the police had done, the invective and calls for more struggle were still daunting.

Emrys conceded that the nine left-wing papers were as vociferous as ever. If you read them you could not help but wonder if the challenges wouldn't go on until the British left. "But I take some comfort in the knowledge that the continuing calls to arms consistently exaggerate what is actually happening."

The frequent dose of bombs real and fake delayed my realization that Emrys was right about driving the leaders underground. The numbers of demonstrators and strikers the communists could bring out into the streets were far less than in May and June. Although the disruption and distress they caused were palpable and went on for months, it was the strikers who were the biggest losers.

A subsequent compilation of strikers dismissed in public transport and utilities companies put the total at 8,755, with more than two-thirds of those being in the bus companies. The leftists did succeed in disrupting public transport, but private vehicles, trucks, cars, and minivans moved in to take up part of the shortfall. Though they were not licensed, both government and the public were content to accept all the help they could get, in whatever form it came.

Hong Kong was a very inconvenient place in mid-summer, with very stringent water rationing and periodic food shortages as well as limited transportation. Now the public was blaming the leftists for all of it. We gave the local Chinese credit for their own version of the British stiff upper lip.

After the Sha Tau Kok incident, the police got much tougher, and at least a half dozen people were shot to death by police in the week after the policemen at the border were killed. Demonstrations were much smaller by that time, with incidents scattered and numbers only in the hundreds. The police confronted these demonstrations with force.

Raids on leftist headquarters were denying the communists places to organize. Police arrested the leaders in their homes and held them under emergency regulations.

By the time of the spectacular August 4 raid it was becoming evident that many leftist organizations were in disarray, but it took only a few people to gather together for a flash demonstration and then scatter in different directions when confronted by the police. It took even fewer to plant a bomb and tie up traffic for hours while the police investigated. Many of these incidents seemed to be the work of small groups of people acting on their own, inspired by exhortations in the pro-communist press.

The bombing campaign seemed to be almost as successful in keeping tension high as the demonstrations and strikes had been earlier. Viewed from the perspective of today's bombings and the carnage they create, the Hong Kong firecracker powder devices were hopelessly ineffective.

Hong Kong people did not see it that way. They were surrounded by Cultural Revolution frenzy and persistent rumors of an impending Chinese takeover.

Adding to Hong Kong's jitters were frequent incidents on the border. The incursions were small: thirty people seizing weapons from a Gurkha soldier and a British officer, 100 more dispersed by tear gas, an agreement to allow Mao posters as long as they weren't incendiary. The British closed the border, except for the Lo Wu train crossing that I had visited. Peking demanded that a new border fence be taken down and the other crossing points be reopened so that Chinese farmers could cross freely to work. PLA troops could be seen from the Hong Kong side, but they did nothing to stop a steady stream of small but unnerving incidents.

CHAPTER 47

Arrests, Attacks, Assassination

THE NINE PRO-COMMUNIST NEWSPAPERS kept spouting incitement. I wondered why the Hong Kong government continued to leave them alone after nearly three months of what could only be called sedition. Emrys explained, "Shutting them down risks an explosive reaction from Peking. You know the government and the communist party own the *Ta Kung Pao* and the *Wen Wei Po*. It's a delicate situation."

After the August 4 raid the communist press screamed "Fascist atrocity!" and called for guerrilla warfare. Even though their shouts were sounding like a paper tiger, they were still worrying people. Finally the government moved against the weakest of the pro-communist newspapers on August 9, arresting key people from three of them and the head of the printing company that served all three. The five people arrested were charged next day with sedition, producing inflammatory reports and spreading false news. Publication of the three papers was suspended several days later. On August 19, police raided the papers when they defied the suspension, making more arrests.

The day after those raids the Chinese Foreign Ministry summoned the British chargé in Peking and demanded immediate release of nineteen jailed left-wing journalists. The note demanded that the suspension of the three newspapers must be canceled within forty-eight hours, or the British would suffer all the consequences.

None of us anticipated the ferocity of those consequences; not Bill Wells or Allen Whiting, not Burt Levin or me or Emrys Davies. We knew that this kind of ultimatum was very unusual in diplomacy, but Peking's relations with other countries were uniformly terrible in the summer of 1967. The language coming out of the Foreign Ministry was antagonistic without precedent for a country not actually at war. Was this serious?

I think it fair to say that we had become somewhat immune to Peking's bluff. We knew that control of the Foreign Ministry had been contested by ultra-radicals for months, but Burt and others believed that Chou En-lai was still capable of keeping the worst from happening, notwithstanding the sacking of the Shanghai residence of the British Consul in May.

We were wrong. A rebel faction had seized control of the Foreign Ministry. Their ultimatum was backed by a Red Guard mob reported to be 10,000 strong gathered outside the British diplomatic compound. When the forty-eight hours passed without British compliance, they broke into the compound, set the chancellery afire, and attacked the diplomats and their families. Ultimately the crowd let them go as the PLA moved in and promised protection, but not before they had done so much damage that Peking later renovated the compound.

Since the events in Peking were in response to the Hong Kong crackdown, I asked Allen Whiting what I should be reporting about it. He gave me one of those intent looks that suggested I should already know the answer to the question. "Doesn't it strike you as a bit strange that we haven't seen much of consequence going on in the streets here while all this violence was vented against the Brits in Peking?" He added that Bill Wells was working on a report that there had also been a big demonstration supporting the Hong Kong compatriots in Canton, "but it's so chaotic there that it's hard to tell what that might have really been about."

Meanwhile, I had heard nothing about border incidents for the past several days. Hong Kong had its bombs, and there were expressions of outrage when two children were killed by one on August 20, but the attack on the British Mission in Peking seemed to be an event particular to itself. It reverberated in Hong Kong as news, but did not spark a new wave of widespread local confrontation.

It all raised the question of Peking's ultimate intentions once again. We could believe that Peking did not intend to take over the colony, but we could only ask who was in charge in Peking, and would those who did not want to see a takeover prevail?

Tension in Hong Kong remained high, even though damage from the ongoing bombing campaign was slight. The latest tactic of a self-styled combat group in Hong Kong was to threaten assassinations. They carried out one, stopping popular anti-leftist Commercial Radio host Lam Bun as he was driving to work on August 24, tossing a gasoline bomb and setting him and his cousin on fire as they tried to get out of the car. The grisly nature of this murder consolidated anti-communist sentiment in a community that had been showing steadily increasing approval for HKG willingness to do whatever it took to stop the communist disruption.

CHAPTER 48

Y.C. Explains

I CALLED ON Y.C. LIANG to see what he thought about all this. He seemed totally at ease in his traditional Chinese scholar's gown, while I felt foolish wearing a suit with fourteen layers of fabric around my neck in Hong Kong's summer heat and humidity. A servant brought tea. Y.C. asked for my thoughts about recent developments. I asked him, *"Cheng nei do-do ji-gau,"* (Please instruct me).

"It is very complicated." He hesitated. "Very complicated. The radical factions took control of the Foreign Ministry or this would not have happened. Chou En-lai had to rely on the army to stop the Red Guards. That is happening in Canton too. Attacking the British Mission was Red Guards out of control. It does not mean that Chou wants to threaten Hong Kong now. He has to be very careful, but he still has power and will have to use it to regain control."

I asked him about reports of troop movements. "The PLA at the border are in plain sight, but they don't stop those small groups that cross over and create trouble. Why not?"

Y.C. said, "This is complicated too. In China, nothing is what it looks like. The PLA needs to be seen as being on the side of the people, so they let these small things happen.

The real purpose of the troops brought up near the border is not to invade Hong Kong, but to keep the Red Guard hotheads out." Having confirmed Bill Wells' speculation, he added that cooler heads in Beijing were keenly aware that Hong Kong was infinitely more valuable to them as a British colony than it would be as a trophy taken over from the so-called imperialists and their running dogs.

CHAPTER 49

Fear and Loathing

Y.C. LIANG'S COMMENTS ASSUAGED some of my concerns but did nothing to relieve the apprehension in Hong Kong. China's ultimatum demanding the release of the arrested journalists, the sacking of the British compound when the HKG refused, and the gruesome murder of Lam Bun left Hong Kong people stirring in a cauldron of fear and loathing. Reports of 100,000 anti-British demonstrators in Canton, PLA troops by the border, and rumors of a takeover in the offing only made worse the toxic brew bubbling with certainty that China could take over Hong Kong any time it wanted and the colonial government could not help the people who wanted to get out.

Some did get out, people I knew or heard about. Quite a few of those very upper-crust friends who had sent their children to study in the US, England, Australia, or Canada took off to visit them for the duration. Others, mostly professionals and businessmen, emigrated to Canada, which welcomed Chinese who had money to invest. A quarter of a million dollars in liquid assets was sufficient to secure a visa for jittery Hong Kong entrepreneurs and their families. Vancouver would come to be known as little Hong Kong.

There wasn't enough time in the day for me to follow the effects of the riots on the economy, and I didn't think that my colleagues in the Economic Section could find clarity in the competing claims until much later. The leftists claimed severe economic damage, while the government put out optimistic reports that the economy was fine. The argument would persist, but without the benefit of a single course in economics, I can tell you the impact of China's Red Guards and the domestic threats on Hong Kong's economy were devastating for some, and deeply personal.

There were things I knew to be true at the time, without the benefit of statistical analysis or hindsight. The local real estate market collapsed. Our Administrative Section chief was housed in a lovely 3,000-square-foot apartment on Conduit Road, a luxurious section of Hong Kong's Mid-Levels between the Central District and the Peak. He reported that a similar flat in his building was offered to him by the neighbor for US$30,000, about a tenth of what it would have sold for before the riots.

The fire-sale status of the real-estate market during the summer of 1967 was a reflection of the fear that hung like low-lying clouds, leaving Hong Kong in a fog of uncertainty about the weather, the economy and the future.

How I wanted to buy that apartment. I was sure that Hong Kong would live to see another day as a British-run paradise for expats like me. Once everybody else believed Hong Kong would survive, it would sell for much more than that $300,000 it could have commanded before the riots. Maybe I would live in it someday. Riots or no, I was still in love with Hong Kong, and I dreamed of having my piece of paradise for a song. The communists weren't going to take it away from me.

It was four years of my salary. Of course I didn't have the money, and there was another hitch even if I did. FSOs were prohibited from investing in the countries where they were serving. Entrepreneurs with the guts to buy those bargains emerged as Hong Kong's biggest real-estate tycoons. Among them was Li Ka-shing, who in 2016 was listed in *Forbes* as Hong Kong's wealthiest man with a net worth of US$31 billion.

CHAPTER 50

Water!

COULD THE HONG KONG GOVERNMENT maintain order in the face of the ongoing bomb campaign and threats of endless struggle? That was still an open question in September, even though the process of disgracing the communists was well underway. The raids, arrests, trials, and the clear threat that their newspapers were no longer a sanctuary for sedition had put them on the defensive. Communist influence in Hong Kong would be greatly reduced for decades to come, but that was still far off. As summer was coming to an end in 1967, I was looking for straws in the wind hinting that the worst of the crisis was over.

From time to time I had asked Emrys Davies whether he had any indication of Chinese intentions about renewing the annual water contract that had alleviated Hong Kong's water shortages since 1960. The heat and humidity were unrelenting and water worry was increasing. Once the typhoon season ended, Hong Kong would receive much less rainfall. It would be impossible to avoid even stricter rationing. Water pressure during the allotted hours of open taps was noticeably less than before, sometimes hardly more than a trickle.

Emrys had told me throughout the summer that the Kwangtung water authorities the HKG used to communicate with on a regular basis were not responding at all now. "The possibility that Hong Kong could be desperately short of water is more worrisome than the bombs. Lack of water promises real suffering." Contingency plans to buy water from Japan and ship it in had been drawn up, but there was no expectation of being able to make up for the shortfall during the dry season.

October 1 was China's National Day. A smattering of Chinese flags could be seen in communist-owned storefronts, but it was hardly a day to celebrate in Hong Kong. When I returned home from work I went to the bathroom, ladled some water from the tub into the sink, soaked a washcloth, and wiped the grime off my face. I stared at the shower curtain and envied what I could not have.

Then I noticed something different. The cold-water faucet in the sink was dripping. It hadn't dripped before. Or I hadn't noticed it. I turned the spigot, almost trembling in anticipation. "Barbara come here. Are you sure it's not our scheduled water hours?"

"Positive." Running water. "Ladies first."

Barbara emptied the brackish water in the bathtub and showered. I could hardly wait.

When she was finished I threw thoughts of saving water to the winds of selfishness. I filled the tub up high and slithered in. Soap down the toes. I had contracted *heung kong jiau*, athlete's foot and fungus toenails. Not as bad as Mr. Farnsworth, who had had his toenails cut off and limped for months afterward, but it was bothersome enough to wash feet first and urge the itching to stop. From there I worked my way up slowly, feeling as if I was removing the whole summer's worth of brine and grime.

I stayed in the bathtub a very long time. Barbara called me several times for dinner. Then she sent Kam-lan to knock on the door and tell me it was getting cold. I stalled and lolled a few more minutes in paradise.

The restoration of the water supply was my watershed in the Hong Kong disturbances. After all the months of riots and bombs and communist threats of annihilation; after my eternity moments with the mob in my face, with the machine-gun in my face, and yes, with the consul general in my face, it all boiled down to this: When I could finally get into a bathtub and loll in the water as long as I wanted; when I could luxuriate in the knowledge that the communists on the other side of the border with China had turned on the tap, I celebrated that sublime feeling of certainty that the People's Republic had no intention of taking back Hong Kong, at least not yet.

CHAPTER 51

Don't Tell Washington Yet

N OT LONG AFTER MY EPIC BATH I got together with
Maynard Parker and Sydney Liu for lunch. They
laughed when I told them that being able to bathe without
remorse meant that the worst was over.

"Could be," said Liu. "But it doesn't look like these bombs
and the attacks on police cars and buses are going to end
until Peking orders the leadership in the New China News
Agency to put a halt to it and stop the incitement."

Maynard rubbed his hand across his chin. I wondered
how Peking's presumed command of events in Hong Kong
could possibly be that clear. Then Maynard spoke up. "It
looks more and more like what's left of the struggle is
random acts of violence from the most radical elements.
There's no telling whether the New China News Agency is
in control any more."

It looked to me like a half-finished puzzle: either the
bomb campaign goes on because the rabble is out of
control, or it is master-minded by the NCNA and nobody
in Peking will order the local communist leadership to stop
because they would be attacked by the same Red Guard

faction that was behind the sacking of the British legation. Same outcome either way.

Maynard mused some more. "It's ironic. If the Hong Kong Chinese had believed that the PRC was really going to march in and take over, most of them probably would have been in the streets waving their Little Red Books and singing praises of Mao. Yet they worry about that all the time, even now. You can't help wondering what might have happened if the communist leaders here had pursued the labor disputes instead of Mao think and gotten more support from Peking. The local population had no love for the colonial government when the riots started. But now they demand even more aggressive police action."

The three of us speculated about that, with different opinions. Like Y.C. said every time I saw him, the situation was very complicated. Then Maynard came up with a compelling thought. "It's China who comes out of this looking like a paper tiger. If the intention was to make Hong Kong into another Macau by humbling the Brits while leaving them in Government House, they failed miserably."

"That's true but it doesn't tell us when the troubles will end."

As we finished eating the sliced oranges that fancy restaurants serve at the end of the meal, I asked Maynard and Sydney Liu if they had time to take a stroll in the area before heading back to our offices. We were on the edge of Wan Chai, and I hadn't walked in the area since the riots began. Victoria Park had been the scene of large demonstrations and confrontations with the police, but there was no hint now that had happened. The only people in the park were mothers with young children and some fast walkers in a hurry to get somewhere else.

The double-decker trams ran serenely down Hennessy Road, screeching when they took the turn leading toward the Happy Valley Race Course. Arcaded old buildings lined the main streets, offering protection on the covered sidewalks when it rained. Side streets were packed with tiny shops offering food, daily necessities, jewelry and trinkets for the visitors who came for the available women, or just to sightsee. Gloucester Road offered a cornucopia of neon signs reaching out from the bars of Suzie Wong fame. Looking up, the sea of unlit neon seemed to be tangled in the web of electric wires connecting poles to buildings across the streets, along the streets, and cattycorner. Humanity crowding the walkways felt intimately connected as we weaved our way among people twisting and turning to get past each other.

No flash demonstrators appeared suddenly in the streets. No bombs cordoned off by police who had to treat fakes as real until proven otherwise. It all appeared so very normal. Sydney Liu pointed out a couple of Land Rovers packed with police, "See how they make sure you can see the carbines." That was different from the Hong Kong I knew before the confrontation.

I couldn't help but think how different Hong Kong rioters were from those who took to the streets in the United States. Detroit had just experienced huge race riots not three months before. It took thousands of National Guard and army troops to quell an urban insurrection. Much of the riot area in Detroit was looted and put to the torch, leaving it an urban wasteland when order was restored after nearly a week.

In Hong Kong property damage after four and half months of communist agitation was insignificant. Comparing the two, it was hard not to think of the Hong Kong confrontation as more a war of words than violence in the streets. But forgive the citizens of Hong Kong for not looking at it that way. It was hard to escape fear of what havoc the Cultural Revolution might wreak on the colony where so many had found refuge from China's turmoils.

Hong Kong breathed a collective sigh of relief with the return of normal water supplies. In my parochial view from the bathtub, continuing disruption by small bands of zealots was nothing compared to the larger meaning of having water from China.

Yet I knew that more water couldn't stop people from having nightmares that the Gurkha regiment and British army units had no hope of defending Hong Kong if the People's Liberation Army decided to take the colony by force.

I went to see Allen Whiting with my thoughts that the worst of the crisis was over. He propped his elbows on his desk, held his head between his knuckles, and thought about this for a bit. Then he smiled. "You are probably right, but I'm not sure it would be wise to trumpet that analysis to Washington just yet. If you turn out to be wrong we all look like fools. Foreign Service people remember that."

CHAPTER 52

Music Reigns Again

A FTER NEARLY HALF A YEAR of incessant turmoil, the disturbances had simmered down to isolated incidents. The six-month suspension of three pro-communist newspapers by the High Court in early September resulted in some softening of leftist rhetoric. More verbiage was devoted to the complexity of the long-term fight against imperialism and less to immediate struggle. There was talk among the reporters who visited that the communist apparatus in the colony was beginning to back down.

I knew Hong Kong would thrive again when music came back into my life with renewed vigor. A call came from Moya Rea, the doyen of Hong Kong pianists and the force behind many of the City Hall Concert Hall recitals by local musicians. "This is last minute but City Hall finally gave permission to Francesca Chan to put on a charity concert next Sunday for the Confucian Academy. She apologized profusely for the short notice and asked if we might do part of her variety program."

"Of course." I was as excited as when Hal Christie arranged that very first concert with the Hong Kong Philharmonic so soon after we arrived. Culture was coming back. I picked some pieces that I knew Moya could master in a minute and practiced my head off. Barbara knew that part of me and came out of the bedroom sometime after 11 p.m. to suggest that I ought to consider the neighbors.

"Our Music Critic" for the *South China Morning Post,* the sometimes quaint Maple Quon, wrote of the concert that Francesca "provided variety too, in her changes of costume for each group of songs, appearing in two evening dresses and a Chinese gown. . . ." With the review came the answer why Moya and I had been invited to perform. We filled in the gaps of a pops concert while Francesca changed her outfits.

That autumn of 1967 I also heard that Zuckermann Harpsichords was producing kits in Greenwich Village and shipping them to aficionados eager to have a modern replica of that ancient keyboard instrument. Though I gave up the piano before I was nine and doubted I would have time to learn the harpsichord, having one would allow me to host baroque music parties. Moya Rea shared my enthusiasm. There weren't any harpsichords in Hong Kong. We ordered two kits shipped half way across the world so we could build instruments that had all but disappeared from concert halls.

By early 1968 Hong Kong's emergency was pretty much behind me. Instead of late nights at the office, I was spending much of my newfound free time gluing the frame, adjusting the soundboard, fitting the pins, stringing the wire strings, carving and fitting the plectra, fashioning the jack springs, adjusting the jacks, putting lead pellets into the ends of the keys to give them enough weight to return after being played; all the things that must be done to create the innards of a harpsichord. Moya's husband Frank had his shipyard carpenters build us superbly crafted mahogany cases for our instruments. I wondered if those craftsmen had been on strike and come back to work just in time to avoid being fired.

Concerts after all those months of confrontation were still exciting. I would get nervous five minutes before going on stage and somehow conquer it by the time I had to play. At my last concert before we were transferred to Taiwan, I played one of my favorite recital pieces, a rarely performed lilting sonata in F composed by a six-year-old. It was the work of the all-time wunderkind, Wolfgang Amadeus Mozart. I don't think the music historians ever established how much if any help the young genius might have gotten from his father. It didn't matter. The kid could light a fire in my belly that has already survived more than twenty-five years longer than my life and love in the Foreign Service.

CHAPTER 53

Dénouement

I HAVE LINGERED LEISURELY and long on my love of music.
That passion has been a thread running through the
entire weave of my life, sometimes barely perceptible,
sometimes dominating all else. It yielded to the excitement
of crisis, and now reclaims its rightful place.

By the end of 1967, I had learned from Y.C. Liang and
other sources that the moderate faction in Peking had
regained enough authority for Chou En-lai to order a
complete halt to any challenges to Hong Kong government
authority. The Cultural Revolution still raged in China,
making for an uneasy calm, but that was the norm with
the border only an hour away.

Communist organizations and their leftist friends had
incurred such enmity that they were kept more or less
outside the pale of society for decades. The British were
learning that their stay in Hong Kong would be only
temporary. Peking would insist that they had to return the
entire colony when the lease on the New Territories expired
in 1997, if not before. That Hong Kong Island and the
Kowloon peninsula had been ceded in perpetuity was

irrelevant. They could not survive either as a British entity or a city-state like Singapore.

Chinese New Year 1968 was calm. The rat-a-tat of incessant firecrackers was nowhere to be heard. Fireworks and the possession of material to make them were still banned. Celebrations were sober, marked by grateful relief that the crisis was over, at least for now. Like other conversations in the spring of 1968, New Year talk almost always turned at some point to Hong Kong's recent turbulent past and uncertain future.

There was no avoiding the fresh nightmares. When the Chinese Cultural Revolution came to Hong Kong, the bearers of Mao thought renamed Caucasians, calling us *baak pei jyu,* white-skinned pigs. Before that, we Westerners were known as *faan gwai lo,* troublesome foreign devils. We could smile at that. But in 1967 we were fascist imperialists facing Chinese rioters inspired by Mao's endless revolution. They took to the streets to show their fealty and vent their spleen against the British colonial government, notwithstanding the fact that half of Hong Kong's people were refugees who had fled from upheavals in communist China.

The rioters gathered in groups large and small for months, waving Mao's little Red Book and shouting *"Wong pei gau!"* at police struggling to control violence, their own fears and the urge to strike back. "Yellow-skinned dogs" were the Chinese who worked for the British colonial administration, and the worst yellow-skinned dogs of all were the police who struggled to maintain order. At times smaller gangs ambushed police patrols with meat hooks.

Fatalities were minor by today's standards of upheaval, but they were no small matter in 1967 Hong Kong. The May riots quickly evolved into a full-scale challenge to government authority, and persisted with demonstrations, homemade bombs, violent clashes with the police, and a seditious propaganda tsunami. Fear that China would take over the colony was pervasive for months. For some, the nightmares would last much longer.

In April 1968 I accepted an invitation from a former Cantonese language school classmate to spend a weekend at a church retreat on Lantau Island, located near the 3,000-foot summit of its highest peak. The hike up and the breeze at the top made for a refreshing getaway from big city life. Missionaries and their guests regularly spent time there, ever since the Methodists built the complex in the 1920s.

A young Chinese man named Lam chatted with me about the experience he didn't know we shared. We sat on the lawn some distance from the cut stone buildings that housed the missionaries, members of their flock, and guests like me. The grass pressing on my jeans hinted at damp. Intense and engaging, Lam told me that his minister had invited him. He said he had never been to the countryside before.

As warm evening settled in, I gazed in wonder at the glittering Hong Kong and Kowloon skyline, almost merging together in the East. To the West, the tiny enclave of Macau came into focus, bringing an image of roulette wheels spinning in the Lisboa Casino that dominated the skyline of the nominally Portuguese colony. They fed the communist fat cats who had taken charge there. A faint glow in the north hinted at Canton hiding in shadow beyond the boats plying the Pearl River estuary. For years it was opium capital of the world.

Four hundred fifty years of symbiotic but often hostile contact between China and the West lay before my eyes. I blinked at the enormity of it. By chance, I was there to feel the geography and pathology of those centuries of trade, war, colonialism and revolution, from the summit of Fung Wong Shan, Lantau Peak.

Lam was no yellow-skinned dog. He was a tough young man who said he was looking for work, with uncertain prospects. He talked freely about his background, how he had been caught up in a movement bent on emulating the chaos that was gripping Mainland China. A year prior to our meeting, he was convinced by the frenzy of the moment that Mao was invincible and the colonialists were pigs to be slaughtered.

Lam revealed that he spent his early years in one of countless squatter shacks crammed into the steep Hong Kong hillsides. "It was very dangerous."

Too often these makeshift communities of refugees were engulfed in mud when typhoons struck. Landslides shredded the flimsy huts, hurling the detritus and walls of water and waste into the streets of Wan Chai and other vulnerable areas of the colony. "I saw what happened when the storms came," he said. "Then the government moved us into the Tung Tau Resettlement Estate."

"That name rings a bell," I said. "Wasn't it the scene of one of the earliest big riots?"

Lam nodded. "It's bad there. The newer estates are better."

He did not carry that look of determined desperation that was so common among Hong Kong's refugees. He wore clean slacks rather than the flimsy pajama-like garment that was standard among refugee laborers. His short-sleeved white shirt was not frayed. He seemed to be relaxed, mirroring the kind of relief from daily drudge found at the retreat.

"How did you come to be related with the church?" I asked in Cantonese.

"If you know anything about living conditions in the estates ... there are many advantages to being in the church."

Like other Chinese I had met, Lam showed no concern about being a Christian in name only. Ron Saucci had told me that they joined for the benefits, often to find respite from a grubby life lived with strangers who barely fit in the room they shared.

After allowing some time for us to get comfortable with each other, I asked Lam if he had participated in the riots.

"We all did. The real riots started right in the resettlement block where I live."

"Oh. Where was that?" I did my best to appear puzzled.

"Tung Tau Resettlement Estate. I told you before."

"What happened there?"

"We decided to show support for the strikers and demonstrate against the pigs who were trying to break it up. At dusk we set fire to trash and some old tires to get it going. Soon we had a big crowd. It's easy because there's always a crowd where I live."

"Tung Tau Resettlement Estate? Just where is that?"
"That's the huge block of rats' nests right by Kowloon City.
You know? Not far from the airport."

"You were there when it all happened?"

Lam looked away for a moment. "Sure. I was one of the
organizers."

I apologized. "I'm just trying to understand and my
Cantonese isn't so good. What happened next?"

"There was this *baak pei jyu*—a British cop who came
into the crowd to spy on us. Except for the missionaries
they're the only whites who come into the estates. They
won't let us make a living. Everybody hawks something on
the street. Food, clothes, lottery tickets, betting the horses
at Happy Valley. Everything. They fine us and keep the
money. The British are even more corrupt than the Chinese
cops. At least we can bargain with Chinese."

"What did you do about the cop at the demonstration?"

"He wasn't in uniform, so we didn't know in the beginning that he was a cop. A couple of us were about to tell
him he shouldn't be here, but he broke and ran so the crowd
surrounded him and started to beat him."

"Why did they do that if they didn't know he was a cop?"

"I told you about the *baak pei jyu*. That's what we called
people who aren't Chinese, and any white-skinned pig that
came into our estates was suspicious. The crowd was angry
and somebody yelled that he was a cop, but they weren't
hitting this guy real hard. He didn't go down."

A chill crept down my spine. I was reliving the story. "It
sounds like he was in real trouble. He must have been
terrified."

"We didn't want any trouble. I was right there and the man was saying over and over again that he's not a policeman but a missionary studying Cantonese."

"He spoke Cantonese?"

"You speak better, but he spoke. A couple of us shouted to the crowd that we should let him go and stay out of trouble. We formed a V and led him away from the demonstration. His shirt was torn but he wasn't really hurt. I watched him going down the street as fast as he could and thought it was a good thing to get him out of there."

Just to be sure, I asked, "And all this happened at the Tung Tau Resettlement Estate last May 11?"

"Yes. I'll never forget it."

My back tingled goosebumps. I would never forget it either.

I looked out towards Hong Kong, anticipating what Lam would say next. Tall skyscrapers dominated the Hong Kong side of the harbor, but shanties held sway on some of the steepest hillsides. I wondered what would keep them from washing down in a river of mud when the next typhoon struck.

On the Kowloon side of the harbor the buildings melted into one another. The airport runway stuck out well into the harbor, clearly visible, allowing me to spot where the Tung Tau Resettlement Estate complex should be, but the buildings were so densely packed that I could not make it out for sure. What daily life was like for Lam and thousands of others allotted twenty-four square feet in a shared warren was almost beyond my imagination.

Lam interrupted my reverie. "That was only the beginning of what happened that evening. We set trash afire, yes,

because the government didn't pick it up, but the demonstration was peaceful.

"It wasn't very long after we let that *baak pei jyu* go that
the police stormed in with their batons flying. They
demanded to know where he was and what we did to him.
We told them what happened. They screamed and cursed
and cracked skulls with their batons. We weren't fighting
back or anything. They just kept beating anyone who
couldn't outrun them as we fled."

Lam's face tightened, as if he was reliving the pain. I asked
him if there were a lot of cops attacking the demonstrators.

"People said they sent in 400 cops looking for their spy.
That missionary pig was a cop for sure." Lam spewed a
stream of what must have been invective, but no one had
ever taught me such venomous vocabulary.

"If we would have caught that (curses) we would have
beaten him to death. We would have killed him."

I struggled to feign calm curiosity and asked, "You would
have killed him?"

"If you saw what those police pigs did to us. They
bloodied everybody. You would have killed him too." Lam
was almost shouting now. Then, calmly, "Yes, we would
have killed him."

I became obsessed with establishing beyond any doubt
that we were reliving the same shared story. I went through
all the details with Lam again: when, where, what, who,
the sequence of events and why he would have killed the
baak pei jyu, confessed missionary, presumed cop that was
Syd Goldsmith.

"Yes, we would have killed him."

Again. We had gone over his story in great detail—twice—and I was certain. I looked him straight in the eye. Voice quivering ever so slightly, "I was that *'baak pei jyu'* you would have killed on May 11, 1967."

Lam's face drained dreary gray, darker than the night's cast of high clouds that stretched out over Hong Kong and its many islands as far as the eye could see. His face at that moment survives as an indelible engraving in my mind still, fifty years later. Only then did I explain that I was a US Foreign Service Officer working at the American Consulate General, not a police spy.

We sat for some time in stunned silence. I wondered what in the universe of fates brought the rescuer turned killer and his lucky intended victim together on this highest hilltop where the landscape of Chinese relations with Westerners for more than 450 years was visible but hidden in the distance, as were the wheels of fortune in Macau's casinos.

Lam finally broke the silence. "I'm glad we didn't find him."

DIAMOND HILL
Memories of growing up in a
Hong Kong squatter village

Feng Chi-shun

CHINA

TOM CARTER

The
Alphabet
of
Vietnam

A novel
by Jonathan
Chamberlain

KING HUI
THE MAN WHO OWNED
ALL THE OPIUM
IN HONG KONG

JONATHAN CHAMBERLAIN

Dateline
Mongolia

AN AMERICAN JOURNALIST IN NOMAD'S LAND

Michael Kohn

THE
EURASIAN
FACE

Kirsteen Zimmern

Dim
Sum
a survival guide

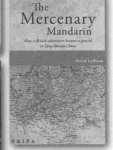

The
Mercenary
Mandarin

How a British adventurer became a general
in Qing-dynasty China

David Leffman

HONG KONG
State of Mind
37 views of a city that doesn't blink

Jason Y. Ng

Walking
the Tycoons'
Rope

ROBERT WANG

Chris Thrall

ONE MAN'S DESCENT INTO
DRUG PSYCHOSIS IN HONG
KONG'S TRIAD HEARTLAND

EATING
SMOKE
A true story

GETTING ALONG
WITH THE
CHINESE
FOR FUN AND PROFIT

Fred
Schnelter

POLICE

SHERIFF OF WAN CHAI
How an Englishman helped govern Hong Kong
in its last decades as a British Colony

PETER MANN

TIBET, THE LAST CRY

Lama of the Gobi

How Mongolia's mystic monks
spread Tibetan Buddhism in
the world's harshest desert

Michael Kohn

The Chinese Wet Market Handbook
A guide to shopping at Hong Kong's fresh food markets

PAM SHOOKMAN

PAPEr
TIGrESS
A LIFE IN THE HONG KONG
GOVERNMENT

RACHEL CARTLAND

HONG KONG
NOIR
FIFTEEN TRUE TALES FROM
THE DARK SIDE OF THE CITY

FENG CHI-SHUN
AUTHOR OF DIAMOND HILL